Doctrine of Rights

Social Justice and The Proofs of God's Existence

by

Dr. ant

Doctrine of Rights: Social Justice and The Proofs of God's Existence

Contents

Chapter 8: Scriptural Basis for Social Justice

Chapter 9: The Role of Grace and Free Will

Chapter 10: Historical Perspectives on Social Justice

Chapter 11: Contemporary Issues in Social Justice

Chapter 12: Practical Applications of Doctrine

Conclusion

Appendix A: Appendix

Glossary of Terms

Introduction

In the annals of history and philosophy, there lies a profound intersection where theology, law, and justice converge. This book seeks to navigate that sacred intersection, elucidating the commonality between Catholic Social Justice and the Apologetics for the existence of God. The audience herein comprises Roman Catholics, theologians, judges, attorneys, and politicians, for whom these intertwined paths hold great significance.

To understand the essence of Catholic Social Justice, one must first grasp the dual tenets of rights and responsibilities. These are not mere concepts but divine endowments that frame the moral imperative of humanity. In Catholic teaching, rights are endowed by God, implying an inherent dignity granted to every individual. Responsibilities, conversely, arise as a moral imperative, demanding that humanity act justly to uphold and protect these divinely bestowed rights.

The dialectic between rights and responsibilities forms the cornerstone of Catholic Social Teaching. One without the other is a hollow vessel. Rights, devoid of corresponding responsibilities, fall into the realm of self-serving individualism. Responsibilities without rights lean toward oppressive moralism. Thus, the synthesis of these two creates a holistic and divine law, that beckons man to a higher ethical standard.

The Church emerges as the steadfast guardian of this moral framework. Across centuries, it has imparted teachings, built upon the foundation of sacred scripture and tradition, to promote a vision of society that upholds social justice. The priestly vocation and the faithful, imbued with these teachings, labor to manifest God's kingdom on earth, a kingdom where justice and love reign supreme.

Within the realm of Catholic apologetics, the existence of God is argued through classical and modern lenses. The ontological, cosmological, and teleological arguments find their basis in ancient theological discourse, yet their relevance extends to contemporary debates about the divine.

Modern perspectives, incorporating developments in science and philosophy, continue to attest to the coherence and plausibility of theistic belief. Thus, apologetics serves as the intellectual scaffolding that supports the moral edifice of rights and responsibilities.

The synthesis of social justice teachings and the apologetics of God's existence offers a profound philosophical foundation. It impels the believer to transcend mere legalistic adherence and delves into the deeper ethical justifications for moral duties. The moral law, written by the Creator upon human hearts, demands recognition of the inherent dignity of each person and the necessity of achieving the common good.

Central to this exploration is the concept of human dignity, which the Church holds as a core principle. Human dignity, derived from being made in the image of God, undergirds the entire framework of Catholic Social Justice. It mandates respect for each individual and calls for the elimination of structures that degrade the human person.

The common good, intricately tied to the notion of human dignity, occupies a vital place in theological and social discourse. It is a multifaceted concept that encompasses the conditions necessary for individuals and communities to flourish. By promoting the common good, the Church advocates for a society that not only respects individual rights but also fulfills communal responsibilities.

Natural law, a venerable philosophical doctrine, underpins many teachings on human rights and moral order. According to this precept, there exists a universal moral law that can be discerned through reason. This natural order aligns with divine will and forms the basis for the advocacy of human rights within Catholic teaching.

The scripture provides a robust foundation for social justice. From the prophetic calls for justice in the Old Testament to the teachings of Christ in the New Testament, the Biblical mandate for justice and social responsibility is clear. These sacred texts guide and inspire the Church's mission to create a just society.

Grace and free will, viewed through theological lenses, further illuminate the interplay between divine aid and human autonomy. Grace, viewed as God's benevolent assistance, empowers individuals to fulfill moral responsibilities. Free will permits moral agency, enabling individuals to choose virtue and thereby attain a higher moral standing.

Historical perspectives reveal the Church's evolving understanding and application of social justice. From the early Church Fathers to the present day, there has been continual development in how these teachings are interpreted and implemented. Each era brings new challenges and insights, contributing to a rich tapestry of doctrinal evolution.

In contemporary times, the Church faces modern social justice challenges that require fresh solutions rooted in timeless teachings. Issues like poverty, environmental degradation, and human rights abuses demand innovative strategies grounded in Catholic doctrine. By addressing these problems, the Church remains a relevant and moral force in the modern world.

Practical applications of doctrine showcase how these teachings translate into action. Case studies and real-world examples illustrate the impact of Catholic social justice principles in various contexts. Whether through community programs, legislative advocacy, or personal moral choices, these applications demonstrate the tangible benefits of living out these doctrines.

This book, thus, serves as a guide and a testament to the integral relationship between Catholic Social Justice and the apologetics for God's existence. It aims to inspire action and contemplation, urging its readers to deepen their understanding of these vital concepts and embody them in their daily lives. Whether one approaches as a believer seeking moral guidance or a scholar in search of philosophical clarity, this exploration seeks to illuminate the path toward a just and righteous society.

Chapter 1: The Framework of Rights and Responsibilities

In the grand tapestry of Catholic Social Teaching, the intricate dance between rights and responsibilities forms a foundational pillar, entwined with threads of divine mandate and human morality. To apprehend this delicate equilibrium, one must venture beyond the mere assertion of entitlements, peering into the ethereal realms where duty and devotion converge. From time immemorial, the Church hath illuminated the path, weaving a narrative wherein rights are not solitary orphans but are ever accompanied by corresponding duties. This sacred ascendency toward justice underscores the verity that every right granted by the Creator is tethered to a profound responsibility, a moral imperative that echoes the eternal law. Thus, the Christian vocation encompasses both the sanctity of individual liberty and the imperative to nurture communal welfare, forging an indelible alliance that mirrors the very essence of our Creator's wisdom and love.

The Concept of Rights in Catholic Social Teaching

The framework of rights and responsibilities within Catholic social teaching encompasses a profound ethical landscape, deeply rooted in theological and moral principles. Indeed, the elucidation of rights in this context springs from an ontological understanding of the human person, reflecting both divine intention and natural law. Within the arcane reaches of Catholic thought, rights are perceived not merely as human constructs or societal agreements, but as divine edicts that ground the very nature of human dignity.

In discerning the concept of rights through the lens of Catholic social teaching, one must traverse the intricate relationship between divine attributes and human existence. Rights, according to this doctrine, are inalienable because they emanate from the imago Dei—the image of God in which every individual is created. This sacred resemblance bestows upon each person certain inviolable rights, which are essential for the fulfillment of their divine purpose. Hence, the safeguarding of these rights is not merely a legal exercise but a spiritual imperative.

It is imperative, then, to explore the teleological aspects of rights in Catholic doctrine. Rights serve as a means to an end, facilitating the human journey toward communion with God and the achievement of ultimate beatitude. The enumeration of rights in papal encyclicals and conciliar documents consistently echoes this metaphysical telos. For instance, the right to life, the cornerstone of all other rights, finds its ultimate justification not solely in its utilitarian benefits but in its alignment with the divine will, which holds human life as sacred.

Moreover, Catholic social teaching accentuates the concept of subsidiarity, which interrelates with the notion of rights. This principle advocates for the respect and empowerment of local and individual capabilities, ensuring that rights are actualized at the most immediate, relevant level. By doing so, it maintains a harmonious societal equilibrium, honoring the rights of individuals while simultaneously fostering communal responsibilities.

In the synthesis of rights, Catholic social teaching also emphasizes the principle of the common good, which transcends individualistic interpretations of rights that often lead to conflicts and fragmentation within society. The common good is articulated as the sum total of conditions allowing individuals and groups to reach their fulfillment more readily and completely. Rights, therefore, must be understood in a communal context, balanced by reciprocal responsibilities to others and to society at large.

This holistic vision extends further into the spheres of economic and social rights, acknowledging the necessity for decent living conditions, fair wages, and access to education and healthcare. The encyclical *Rerum Novarum* and its successors, including *Quadragesimo Anno* and *Centesimus Annus*, delineate a robust defense of workers' rights, underscoring that labor is not merely a commodity but an expression of human dignity and participation in God's creative work. Thus, the dignity of labor becomes a paramount right, safeguarded against exploitation and injustice.

Education, as explicated in Catholic documents, transcends mere intellectual acquisition; it is a fundamental right that enables individuals to develop their God-given talents and fulfill their vocation. Similarly, healthcare, rooted in the preferential option for the poor, is viewed as a right intrinsic to the sanctity of life. These rights are not abstract ideals but mandates demanding concrete actions from both individuals and institutions, resonating with the Church's mission to manifest divine justice and love in the temporal realm.

The interplay between individual rights and communal responsibilities extends to the environmental domain, as articulated in *Laudato Si'*. Pope Francis eloquently argues that the right to a healthy environment is inextricable from the rights of individuals and communities to live in harmony with Creation. This ecological dimension introduces a necessary balance, reminding the faithful that rights must be exercised with a conscientious stewardship of God's creation, reflecting a cosmic solidarity that encompasses present and future generations.

Integral to this discourse is the moral theology underpinning rights, grounded in the natural law tradition. This tradition asserts that certain rights are self-evident, discernible through reason and consonant with human nature. Aquinas' exposition of natural law serves as a foundation, where rights are not arbitrary but reflective of a divinely ordered reality. Rights and moral duties are thus two sides of the same coin, ensuring that one's exercise of rights does not infringe upon the rights of others.

Furthermore, the defense of human rights finds expression in the Catholic Church's social activism and advocacy. The Church has consistently championed the rights of marginalized and oppressed groups, drawing upon its rich doctrinal heritage to challenge systemic injustices. The preferential option for the poor underscores this commitment, advocating for those whose rights are most vulnerable. This preferential option calls for a transformation that goes beyond mere charity, demanding structural changes to create a just society where every person's rights are upheld.

The concept of rights in Catholic social teaching is not static but dynamic, responding to the evolving realities of human society while rooted in immutable divine truths. This dynamism is evident in the Church's engagement with contemporary issues such as digital privacy, bioethics, and global migration, adapting its timeless principles to address new challenges. The Church's magisterial teachings continue to offer profound insights into how rights can be protected and promoted in diverse contexts, always with an eye toward the universal common good and the glory of God.

To encapsulate, the concept of rights in Catholic social teaching is comprehensive and deeply interwoven with the Church's mission to uphold human dignity and promote justice. It integrates theological, philosophical, and moral dimensions, offering a coherent vision that transcends secular understandings of rights. This vision challenges believers and societies alike to recognize and respect the divine origin of rights, fostering a culture that reflects the Kingdom of God.

In summation, the Catholic Church's articulation of rights is both profound and practical, serving as a beacon of divine truth and moral guidance in an often fractured world. As the faithful navigate the complexities of contemporary society, the Church's teachings on rights offer not only a framework for ethical living but a call to witness to the transformative power of God's love and justice.

Responsibilities as a Moral Imperative

Within the hallowed chambers of Catholic Social Teaching, the covenant of responsibilities assumes a grandeur parallel to the reverence afforded to rights. Responsibilities are not mere appendages to rights; rather, they coalesce into a sine qua non of moral existence. Herein lies a profound truth, that to possess a right is to be encumbered also with a moral duty. For it is a tenet that rights and responsibilities are the dual pillars upon which the edifice of social justice stands, as firm as the foundations of ancient cathedrals. Indeed, our discernment of rights would be impoverished were we to neglect their obligatory counterparts.

When we speak of responsibilities as a moral imperative, we enter a sanctified realm where the weight of conscience and the dictates of divine law converge. Responsibilities are not optional doctrines, but rather imperatives that imprint upon the soul a celestial charge. In embracing these duties, one participates in a grand schema of divine orchestration. Without the acknowledgment of moral duties, rights become hollow, akin to the chiming of bells deprived of their clappers. This interdependency is central to Catholic thought, for how could one claim the sanctity of life while shunning the duty to protect and cherish it?

The moral imperative of responsibilities is deeply woven into the sacramental life of the Church. Through the Eucharist, the faithful are reminded of Christ's ultimate sacrifice—a paradigmatic responsibility undertaken for the redemption of humanity. It is an eternal reminder that genuine love manifests itself in the form of duty and obligation. In the hallowed texts of Scripture, we find a panoply of exhortations urging believers to fulfill their responsibilities with zeal and sincerity. The epistles of St. Paul, for instance, resonate with calls to bear one another's burdens, thereby fulfilling the law of Christ.

Why, then, must we regard responsibilities as these inviolable imperatives? It is because they sculpt the moral character of society, shaping it into a reflection of divine justice. Responsibilities compel us to transcend the narrow confines of self-interest and to act in the service of the common good. They press upon us the urgency of justice and love, demanding that we mirror the boundless mercy of God in our communal lives.

Consider the familial unit, that microcosm of societal order. Parents are invested with the responsibility to nurture and educate their children in the ways of faith and moral rectitude. This duty is not a mere social expectation but a sacred obligation that contributes to the moral fiber of society. Likewise, children bear the responsibility to honor and respect their parents, grounding familial relationships in a mutual exchange of love and duty. Such responsibilities, when embraced wholeheartedly, render the family a bastion of moral and spiritual fortitude.

Within the broader tapestry of human society, political and judicial figures hold positions of power undergirded by immense responsibilities. Judges, attorneys, and politicians must exercise their roles with a profound sense of duty towards justice, equity, and the common good. Their responsibilities are not to be taken lightly, for they are charged with the imperative to uphold the dignity of every human person. The notion of subsidiarity, central to Catholic Social Teaching, directs those in power to act with humility and prudence, ensuring that decisions benefit the least advantaged.

The convergence of rights and responsibilities reaches its apogee in natural law, which itself is a reflection of divine wisdom imprinted upon creation. Natural law reveals to us that duties exist not in isolation but as integral components of a moral order that transcends human law. Through natural law, we comprehend that the pursuit of justice is an innate duty, a moral imperative inscribed upon the hearts of all men and women. Thus, rights vested by natural law are intrinsically linked to corresponding responsibilities, revealing a harmonious interplay of divine mandates.

Moreover, the theological underpinnings of responsibilities as a moral imperative lead us inexorably towards the concept of human dignity. Human dignity, as articulated by the Magisterium, is the bedrock upon which both rights and responsibilities stand. It is a manifestation of the imago Dei, the image of God in which all humans are created. To uphold human dignity, individuals are called to recognize and act upon their responsibilities towards one another. This recognition fosters a culture of life, where the vulnerable are protected, and the world reflects the divine order intended by the Creator.

In this light, moral responsibilities extend beyond the individual to encompass the collective actions of communities and nations. The encyclicals of the Church, such as "Rerum Novarum" and "Laudato Si'", articulate a vision where economic and social structures align with the moral priorities of justice and the common good. These documents call upon nations to assume their responsibilities towards environmental stewardship, social equity, and global solidarity. In every action and policy, responsibilities are to be seen not as burdens but as expressions of communal love and fidelity to divine law.

Consequently, to regard responsibilities as mere formalities or secondary concerns is to misunderstand their true nature. They are the lifeblood of moral society, infusing every action with purpose and direction. With responsibilities firmly grasped, we approach the manifestation of the Kingdom of God on Earth, where justice flows like a river and righteousness like an ever-flowing stream.

Thus, in summation, the framework of rights and responsibilities is incomplete without recognizing the moral imperatives that responsibilities entail. They are woven intricately into the fabric of Catholic Social Teaching, demanding earnest and constant engagement. Through this engagement, we heed the call to be co-creators with God in the pursuit of a just and loving society. The responsibilities we bear are markers of our shared humanity and our divine calling, leading us ever closer to the ultimate fulfillment of justice and peace in the world.

Chapter 2: Understanding Social Justice in Catholic Doctrine

To delve into the essence of Social Justice within Catholic Doctrine, one must first comprehend it as an inherent part of a divine panorama, where rights and responsibilities are inextricably bound by moral law. This justice, transcendent yet grounded, speaks to the ordered symmetry of human relations, both individually and collectively. It is the Church's solemn charge to promulgate this justice, through teachings that appeal to the conscience and seek the common good. At its heart lies a vision of equity, where the dignity of every soul is uplifted, and the miseries of the downtrodden find redress. Herein, justice unfolds not merely as a social contract but as a moral mandate, animated by the love of neighbor and the omnipresent hand of Providence. Thus, in this sacred economy, Social Justice emerges as both a theological virtue and a practical necessity, calling upon the Church to be the harbinger of a just society forged in the eternal truths of divine wisdom.

Social Justice Defined

To traverse the rich tapestry of Catholic doctrine is to encounter a profound dedication to the principles of social justice. This salient tenet, nestling within the sanctified corpus of ecclesiastical teachings, embodies a multifaceted concept blending moral, philosophical, and theological dimensions. Social justice is not an abstract or enigmatic notion; rather, it is a clarion call for a harmonized existence anchored in divine law and human dignity.

The Church fathers, both ancient and contemporary, offer a thesis that social justice is intrinsically tied to the fabric of our collective human duty and the inherent rights bestowed upon every individual by God. In essence, social justice ensures that the moral architecture of society aligns with the divine will. This alignment is facilitated through the promotion of equality, fair distribution of resources, and the safeguarding of human rights.

Given the context of Catholic doctrine, social justice represents a covenant between divine imperatives and human actions. This covenant finds its roots in the sacred scriptures and theological traditions, harmonizing the moral imperatives underscored in Catholic social teaching.

It is essential, then, to fathom that social justice in Catholicism is not merely an attempt to address worldly iniquities; it delves deeper, aspiring to sculpt a society wherein each soul is accorded its rightful dignity as a child of God. As Thomas Aquinas posited, justice is the perpetual and constant will to render each his due. It applies not just to legal matters but to the very ethos of societal interactions.

One cardinal aspect of social justice is its insistence on the preferential option for the poor and vulnerable. This principle emanates from Christ's teachings, reflecting a divine injunction to place the marginalized at the heart of our social and economic systems. In doing so, the Church calls for an active engagement in transforming social structures that perpetuate inequity.

Various encyclicals and papal pronouncements have explicated this vision. Pope Leo XIII's *Rerum Novarum* laid the groundwork for modern Catholic social thought, emphasizing the rights of workers and the responsibilities of both employers and the state. Subsequent pontiffs have built on this foundation, further elucidating the principles of solidarity, subsidiarity, and the common good.

Solidarity, in particular, underscores the unity that should bind the human family. It is a call to transcend personal and communal egoism, recognizing that the flourishing of one is inextricably linked to the flourishing of all. This principle is characterized by a moral obligation to commit to the common good and to advocate for those who suffer injustice.

Subsidiarity, on the other hand, advocates for the empowerment of local communities and institutions. It posits that matters ought to be handled by the smallest, lowest, or least centralized authority capable of addressing them effectively. This principle is essential in combatting the overreach of central authorities and in fostering a sense of agency within communities.

Moreover, the principle of the common good, which permeates much of Catholic social teaching, proposes that societal institutions and policies should be oriented towards what is beneficial for all members of society. It is a call for policies that do not merely cater to the interests of the powerful or the wealthy, but rather seek to uplift the entire community, especially its most disenfranchised members.

The Church's role in promoting social justice is indeed pivotal. It acts as a moral compass, guiding believers to engage in acts of mercy, both corporal and spiritual. Envisioning a society saturated with righteousness and love, the Church implores its followers to be active participants in creating structures that reflect God's justice.

Theologically, social justice is rooted in the Biblical narrative. The scriptures resonate with calls for justice, urging the faithful to act in ways that reflect God's kingdom on Earth. From the prophetic literature of the Old Testament to the parables of Jesus, the divine mandate is unwavering: to act justly, love mercy, and walk humbly with God.

Through the lens of Catholic social teaching, social justice is not merely a policy agenda but a spiritual mission. It is the manifestation of Christ's love in the public sphere, a tangible expression of the Gospel in action. This mission calls for a continual examination of personal and collective consciences, urging the faithful to engage in the transformative work of social justice.

In closing, defining social justice within Catholic doctrine requires an understanding of its divine origins and its practical applications. It embodies the conviction that every person, created in the image and likeness of God, possesses an inalienable dignity that demands respect and defense. This principle, when embraced, directs the community of believers to actively participate in the construction of a society marked by compassion, equity, and justice for all.

The Role of the Church in Promoting Social Justice

In the labyrinth of Catholic thought, the Church holds not just a spiritual mandate but also a tangible, social one. One might ponder, whence does this dual responsibility emerge? It is this question which must be answered, that we may fully appreciate the Church's pivotal role in fostering social justice, a concept deeply embedded in Catholic doctrine.

The Catholic Church's mission extends beyond the salvation of souls; it encompasses the very fabric of worldly existence. Drawing from the sacred texts and lasting traditions, the Church behooves itself to not merely preach but to act, embodying the virtues of justice and charity. We find in its actions a model of active participation in societal affairs, a construction of the common good, which benefits all of humanity.

Consider the Church's interpretation of social justice as configured in the lens of divinely inspired scriptures. Herein, justice finds not a static definition but rather a dynamic, evolving interpretation that aligns with the exigencies of time. Pope Leo XIII's seminal encyclical, *Rerum Novarum*, inaugurated what we might call the modern Catholic social teaching, addressing the then-emerging social disparities resultant from industrialization. His treatise offered a foundational blueprint, elucidating the equal dignity of workers and their rights to fair wages and humane working conditions.

Fast forward to the present, and the Church continues to wield its doctrinal influence in contemporary issues. It speaks fervently against the evils of economic inequality, environmental degradation, and social alienation. Through encyclicals like Pope Francis' *Laudato Si'*, the Church roars with moral fervor against the exploitation of our common home—the Earth— thus interlinking environmental stewardship with social justice.

The Church's role is not restricted to high-level proclamations but pervades the community level, engaging in numerous charitable endeavors. Parishes, dioceses, and Catholic organizations administer aid to the impoverished, the marginalized, and those forgotten by society's indifferent gaze. The Corporal Works of Mercy—feeding the hungry, sheltering the homeless, visiting the sick—are not mere acts of charity but profound expressions of justice, fulfilling Christ's mandate to love one's neighbor as oneself.

One finds in Catholic doctrine a tripartite emphasis on the dignity of the individual, the value of community, and the overriding necessity of the common good. The Church, through its manifold institutions, creates a tapestry of social services and advocacy efforts that resonate profoundly within local and global contexts. Schools, hospitals, and social welfare agencies exemplify the Church's commitment to an equitable society, each functioning as a microcosm of divine justice on Earth.

Politically, the Church wields substantial influence, although it remains a delicate balance between spiritual leadership and temporal intervention. Ecclesiastical leaders, while generally eschewing partisan politics, do not hesitate to offer moral guidance on legislation that impacts social welfare. They lobby for laws that promote equality, campaign against practices that demean human dignity such as human trafficking and abortion, and provide a moral compass in the murky waters of political expediency.

Historically, the Church has stood as a stalwart advocate for civil rights. One need look no further than its participation in the abolition of slavery, the labor rights movements, and civil rights marches. Figures such as Archbishop Óscar Romero and Mother Teresa exemplify the Church's capacity to inspire collective and individual action towards an ethical and just society.

Yet, do not misconstrue the Church's involvement as merely reactionary. It forges societal norms through proactive education and formation, nurturing minds and hearts in schools and seminaries where Catholic social teaching is an integral part of the curriculum. Through catechesis, believers are imbued with a robust understanding of their ethical responsibilities, thus equipping them to pursue justice in their personal, professional, and communal lives.

It is worth noting that the Church understands social justice as inherently linked to personal virtue. The pursuit of justice is not a matter of mere external compliance but an inward transformation, aligning one's will with divine law. This integration of faith and action, belief and practice, is the bedrock upon which genuine social justice is built.

Moreover, the Church's promotion of social justice transcends religious boundaries, engaging in interfaith and secular efforts alike. Its institutions often partner with non-Catholic entities to amplify their impact, demonstrating that the quest for justice is a universal human endeavor, blessed by divine mandate but open to all of goodwill.

In this synthesis of doctrine and deed, the Church showcases a remarkable harmony between the spiritual and societal, the divine and the human. It is an enduring beacon, guiding the faithful and the wider community towards a world that mirrors the Kingdom of God in its justice, peace, and love.

Thus, the role of the Church in promoting social justice is far from being a peripheral concern; it lies at the very heart of its mission. Through its teachings, actions, and relentless advocacy, the Church sustains a living tradition of social justice that continues to inspire, challenge, and transform the world.

Chapter 3: The Existence of God in Catholic Apologetics

Pondering the nexus of divine existence within the vast expanse of Catholic apologetics, one must traverse the woven expanse of both metaphysical contemplations and doctrinal affirmations. The Catholic scholar, armed with the intellectual armament of saints and ecclesiastical minds, engages in a dialectical odyssey. Herein lies the endeavor to illuminate a fundamental axiom—that the existence of God is an immutable truth underpinning the very essence of reality and morality. Through ancient treatises echoing the logic of causality, the ontological necessities, and teleological intricacies, as well as through poignant modern discourse steeped in existential realism and empirical scrutiny, the apologist beckons the wayfarer towards a recognition of the Divine as the uncaused cause. Thus, the existence of God is not merely a matter of forlorn faith but is elucidated and defended through rigorous, reasoned argumentation, interweaving the rich tapestry of tradition and reason to fortify the soul against the tempests of skepticism and indifference.

Classical Arguments for God's Existence

In the vast and storied annals of Catholic Apologetics, the classical arguments for God's existence stand as beacons of philosophical and theological discernment. These arguments, meticulously forged through the combined brilliance of ancient and medieval scholars, offer enduring testimonies to the divine mystery. Within these sacrosanct corridors of reasoning, the faithful find refuge, while the skeptical stand challenged. Let us proceed with an examination, serene yet profound, into this illustrious domain.

Foremost among these venerable arguments is the Cosmological Argument, which elegantly evokes the principle of causality. It begins with the simple, almost axiomatic observation: every event has a cause. In a grand tapestry of contingent events, the argument unfurls a quest for an uncaused first cause, which Catholics unwaveringly recognize as God. This principle, ingeniously articulated by St. Thomas Aquinas in his Quinque Viae (Five Ways), posits that the chain of causality cannot regress infinitely. Rather, it necessitates a prime mover, an uncaused cause, embedding within the cosmos a reflection of divine essence.

The journey from movement to the unmoved mover demands our utmost intellectual rigor and humility. By acknowledging the limits of finite causality, we ascend to an infinite actuality, blinding in its perfection and utterly necessary in its existence. The cosmological reflection is not mere abstraction; it synergizes with the empirical reality, framing divine orchestration in the very fabric of existence.

Proceeding hence, we encounter the Teleological Argument, or the Argument from Design. At its heart, this argument discerns an intelligent purpose woven into the structure of the universe. The intricacy and purpose evident in natural phenomena suggest a grand designer. Aquinas again contributes to our understanding, asserting that natural beings, lacking intelligence, achieve their end by design rather than chance.

The world abounds with examples: the symmetrical intricacies of snowflakes, the precision of planetary orbits, and the complex interdependencies of ecosystems. These marvels do not result from random occurrence but hint at a supremely wise artificer whose hand guides all toward harmonious ends. The argument from design thus resonates deeply, affirming the intuitive recognition of divine craftsmanship in nature's order.

Subsequent to teleology, the Ontological Argument tenderly impels the investigator to contemplative heights. St. Anselm of Canterbury, in his Proslogion, posited that God, being defined as "that than which nothing greater can be conceived," must exist both in the mind and in reality. For the very concept of God, in its maximal greatness, precludes non-existence. Anselm's argument is not without its critics, yet its audacious leap from conception to actuality captivates the metaphysical imagination.

To grasp the ontological argument is to tread the delicate border between language and being, where the intellect must stretch beyond its accustomed bounds. It urges a recognition of God's limitless nature, a sublime existence surpassing all mundane contingencies.

The Moral Argument, articulated with lucidity by Immanuel Kant, yet foreshadowed by earlier Christian philosophers, confronts us with the imperative of moral law. Kant suggests that the existence of an objective moral order, which obliges us universally, necessitates a moral lawgiver. This argument finds fertile ground in Catholic thought, which affirms conscience as the voice of God within. Conscience, though often erring, points unfailingly towards the Good, implicating a source beyond subjective inclinations.

Indeed, the ubiquity of moral recognition across cultures and epochs intimates a divine legislator. The profound sense of moral obligation, felt in the depths of human spirit, cannot be satisfactorily explained by evolutionary survival alone. It is, rather, a signpost of divine order within the human heart.

Lastly, the Argument from Religious Experience extends a personal dimension to our enquiry. The ineffable encounters with the divine experienced by saints, mystics, and ordinary believers alike provide compelling subjective evidence for God's existence. Though such experiences defy empirical scrutiny, they offer transformative power to those who behold them. St. Teresa of Ávila's visions and St. John of the Cross's mystical poems unveil an inner realm where the soul communes directly with the divine. These mystical experiences, while individual in nature, converge upon a transcendent reality that is universally acknowledged within the Church.

It is noteworthy that the cumulative force of these classical arguments does not compel belief through mere rationality but invites it through a synergy of intellect and faith. They are like varied yet harmonious notes, crafting a symphony that echoes the divine mystery within the human soul. Each argument, whether from causality, design, morality, or mystical encounter, offers a distinct yet convergent pathway towards the divine presence.

These classical arguments are enduring pillars within the broader edifice of Catholic apologetics. They guide the intellect through reason, affirming what the heart perceives in faith. Thus, the Church, in her wisdom, nurtures these arguments, strengthening the faithful and illuminating the way for seekers of truth. In the firmament of Catholic thought, they shine as ever-radiant stars, guiding us towards the Almighty.

Modern Perspectives on God's Existence

The challenge of articulating the existence of God has occupied the minds of theologians and philosophers for centuries. In contemporary times, this endeavor has not diminished in importance but has rather taken on new dimensions and intricacies. The modern perspectives on God's existence within the ambit of Catholic apologetics diverge from traditional arguments, engaging with scientific advancements, existential inquiries, and pluralistic dialogues.

Modern Catholic apologetic discourse encounters a world where empirical evidence and scientific methodologies reign supreme. Yet, this encounter need not be adversarial. On the contrary, many apologists find harmony between science and faith, positing that the order and complexity seen in the natural world point to an intelligent Creator. The dialogue with science extends beyond mere compatibility, often engaging with cosmology, quantum physics, and biology to unveil the signs of divine orchestration. Francis Collins and his work at the intersection of genetics and divinity serve as a luminous example of such harmonious inquiry.

Furthermore, existential philosophy provides a fertile soil for modern perspectives on God's existence. The human quest for meaning, purpose, and identity in an often chaotic and indifferent universe leads many to philosophical arguments that resonate with theistic beliefs. This is vividly illuminated in the existential musings of philosophers grappling with questions of authenticity, freedom, and ultimate concern. Søren Kierkegaard's reflections on faith and the paradox of the infinite are seminal in revealing the inextricable link between human consciousness and the divine.

As society moves towards increased pluralism and secularism, Catholic apologists engage with diverse worldviews, aiming to showcase the universality and relevance of theistic belief. Interfaith dialogues and comparative theology reveal the shared pins of morality, transcendence, and quest for the ultimate truth across religious traditions. This engagement not only fortifies Catholic claims but also displays a respectful consideration of other spiritual paths, fostering a conducive environment for theological exchange.

In this rich tapestry of modern perspectives, personal narratives and testimonies provide a compelling and intimate dimension. The experiential aspect of faith—the encounter with the divine in the personal and communal journey—grounds abstract arguments with tangible, lived realities. These stories attest to the transformative power of divine interaction, elucidating a God who is not distant but deeply involved in the human predicament.

Concurrently, modern apologetics must address the prevalent skepticism and atheism characteristic of contemporary discourse. The New Atheism movement, with figures like Richard Dawkins and Christopher Hitchens, challenges the intellectual credibility of theism, often painting it as antithetical to reason and progress. In response, apologists like Alister McGrath and G.K. Chesterton have articulated robust defenses that juxtapose atheistic critiques with nuanced theological reasoning. These engagements elucidate the rational coherence and existential appeal of theistic belief in a secular epoch.

Another notable area of modern apologetic discourse is the ethical and moral argument for God's existence. In an era where moral relativism often prevails, apologists argue that objective moral values and duties necessitate a transcendent grounding. This moral argument posits that without a divine lawgiver, moral imperatives lose their binding force and universality. Ethical frameworks within Catholic doctrine, emphasizing human dignity and social justice, find their ultimate justification in the divine nature, as opposed to contingent societal constructs.

Additionally, the problem of evil and suffering remains a profound challenge to theistic belief, often exacerbated in the modern context by global crises and profound injustices. Apologists address this conundrum by delving into theodicy, exploring how free will, soul-making, and redemptive suffering offer plausible explanations within a theistic framework. The cross of Christ stands central in Catholicism as a symbol of God's solidarity with human suffering, offering hope and meaning amidst affliction.

Intellectual humility and openness to mystery characterize the modern Catholic approach, recognizing that finite human understanding is intrinsically limited when grappling with the infinite. Apologists often invoke the analogy of being, emphasizing an important distinction between God's incomprehensibility and human attempts at articulation. This approach promotes a sense of reverence and awe, encouraging believers to embrace the mysterious yet revealed nature of the divine.

Philosophical inquiry, scientific exploration, existential reflection, and moral reasoning converge in contemporary Catholic apologetics to affirm the coherence and vitality of belief in God. These modern perspectives do not dismiss traditional arguments but build upon them, engaging with the intellectual currents and existential dilemmas of the present age. In doing so, they illuminate the enduring relevance of God's existence, inviting both believers and skeptics to explore the profound depths of faith and reason.

Chapter 4: Linking Rights and Responsibilities with Apologetics

To traverse the nexus where the august principles of rights and responsibilities entwine with the venerable discipline of apologetics, one must first scrutinize the sinews binding them inextricably. This chapter embarks on an intellectual voyage, examining how these pillars of Catholic Social Justice and theological apologism converge, revealing the divine impetus behind both moral duty and the logical defense of God's existence. We venture forth to delineate the philosophical substratum that asserts human obligations as not mere sociopolitical constructs but rather as divinely orchestrated imperatives. Such a foundation posits that each right bestowed upon us is conjoined with commensurate responsibilities, ordained by the Creator, whose existence is rigorously defended by apologetic discourse. In this interplay, the moral fabric—woven from respect for human dignity and divine law—finds its apotheosis, as rights and duties emerge as reflections of an eternal moral order, reinforced by reasoned faith. Together, they eloquently affirm that our responsibilities are not simply codified by human consensus but are imbued with transcendental significance that apologetics tirelessly elucidates.

Philosophical Foundations of Rights and Responsibilities

In the grand tapestry of moral thought, the philosophical underpinnings of rights and responsibilities are threads that weave through the fabric of human existence. Within the domain of Catholic social teaching, these concepts are not merely abstractions but are imbued with profound theological significance. To discern the essence of rights and responsibilities, one must delve into a multifaceted discourse, wherein metaphysical principles, ethical precepts, and divine ordinances coalesce.

The notion of rights, as apprehended within Catholic doctrine, is inextricably linked to the concept of human dignity. Each soul, fashioned in the divine image, is endowed with intrinsic worth. This theological anthropology asserts that the imago Dei confers upon every person a set of inviolable rights. Rights, therefore, are not human constructs but divine endowments that reflect God's own justice and goodness. To grasp this fully is to engage with a metaphysical landscape that recognizes the sacredness of the human condition.

Yet, rights devoid of corresponding responsibilities would render the moral order incomplete. In Catholic thought, human freedom must be exercised in the service of truth and goodness. Responsibilities are the moral imperatives that bind rights to ethical action. Herein lies a symbiotic relationship: without the ethical constraints imposed by responsibilities, rights could devolve into selfish entitlements bereft of moral compass. Thus, responsibilities are seen as the guardians that ensure the proper exercise of rights.

The elucidation of this linkage finds resonance in the natural law tradition, foundational to Catholic moral philosophy. Natural law, a central pillar in the teachings of Church Fathers and Doctors, postulates a universal moral order discernible through reason. This order originates from the eternal law, the divine wisdom governing the cosmos. Through participation in this eternal law, humans derive both rights and duties, embedded in their very nature and revealed through rational inquiry. The fabric of natural law is interwoven with moral norms that uphold justice, instilling both the duty to respect others' rights and the imperative to fulfill one's responsibilities.

However, the framework of rights and responsibilities transcends mere philosophical speculation; it is imbued with theological gravity. Consider the Beatitudes, Christ's blueprint for a life steeped in righteousness. These divine pronouncements reveal a call to embody virtues that inherently balance rights with responsibilities. The blessed who thirst for righteousness are those committed to justice, recognizing their own rights while ardently defending those of their brethren. This mutual recognition forms the bedrock of social harmony and divine justice.

The intertwining of rights and responsibilities also finds expression in the virtue of prudence. Prudence, the charioteer of virtues, guides the moral agent in discerning the appropriate means to fulfil righteous ends. It requires a careful balancing act—ensuring that one's exercise of rights does not trample upon the rights of others, while simultaneously prompting the fulfillment of one's own responsibilities. In this virtue, we see a microcosm of the delicate interplay between individual prerogatives and collective obligations.

Moreover, theological reflection on the Eucharist— the source and summit of Christian life—further illuminates this interconnection. In the Eucharistic celebration, the faithful partake in the Body and Blood of Christ, signifying a profound unity with Him and with one another. This sacramental union underscores a communal ethic where rights are cherished, and responsibilities are undertaken, reflecting the self-giving love of Christ. The Eucharist, then, becomes a paradigm of lived justice, where the faithful are called to mirror the sacrificial love of the Savior in their relational duties.

To encapsulate the philosophical foundations of rights and responsibilities is to engage with a holistic view of human flourishing. Saint Thomas Aquinas, in his magnum opus, *Summa Theologica,* elucidates that the ultimate end of human existence is the beatific vision— the direct encounter with God. In this teleological framework, rights and responsibilities are not mere temporal concerns but are oriented towards the eternal destiny of the soul. They serve as pathways, guiding the moral agent toward the ultimate good.

Furthermore, the patristic writings offer rich, illustrative insights into the lived experience of early Christians, who embodied a profound sense of communal responsibility while ardently defending individual rights. The communal life described in the Acts of the Apostles, where believers held all things in common, underlines a collective responsibility to ensure the welfare of each member. This early Christian community, inspired by the teachings of Christ, practiced a radical form of justice that transcended personal entitlements for the common good.

In contemporary discourse, these philosophical foundations continue to provide a robust framework for addressing modern challenges in social justice. The interplay between rights and responsibilities can be a lens through which contemporary issues are examined, offering solutions grounded in timeless principles. For example, the principle of subsidiarity, integral to Catholic social teaching, posits that social and political decisions should be made at the most immediate level possible. This principle respects individual rights while fostering communal responsibilities, ensuring that higher authorities intervene only when necessary to uphold justice.

Moreover, this philosophical groundwork informs the Church's stance on various socio-political issues, such as immigration and economic inequality. By rooting the dialogue in the intrinsic worth of every person and the corresponding duties to one another, the Church advocates policies that respect individual rights while addressing systemic injustices. The ethical balance between rights and responsibilities thereby serves as a compass, guiding both personal conduct and public policy.

In conclusion, the philosophical foundations of rights and responsibilities within Catholic teachings reflect a deeply interconnected moral vision. Grounded in the theological anthropology of imago Dei, articulated through the natural law tradition, and lived out in the sacramental life of the Church, these concepts are more than theoretical constructs. They are vital precepts that guide human interaction, social justice, and ultimately, the path towards eternal communion with God. To understand and embrace these foundations is to participate in the divine order, aligning one's life with the transcendent principles of justice and love.

Apologetic Justifications for Moral Duties

A keen observer of human experience might meditate upon the very essence of moral duties and their divine origin. Within the context of Catholic Social Teaching, moral duties are not merely social contracts or arbitrary norms; they reside deeply within the bosom of divine law and revelation.

The heart of our reflection must consider how moral duties, viewed through the apologetic lens, are justified as emanations of God's will. These duties are neither capricious nor unfounded but are manifestations of God's immutable nature and His ultimate benevolence towards humanity. Such duties arise from a source that transcends human invention, thereby possessing an objectivity that secures their universality and unaltered constancy.

Philosophers and theologians alike have long discoursed upon the nature of moral duties, often aligning them with the divine will. Thomas Aquinas, for instance, posits that human reason, in communion with divine revelation, can apprehend the foundational precepts of the natural law. This law, discernible by the light of reason, reveals the moral imperatives that God has inscribed upon the human heart, binding every person to a moral order reflective of divine wisdom.

The apologetic enterprise thus necessitates a demonstration of the divine source and rationale of these moral duties. The argument here unfolds as one proving the existence of God through the manifestation of moral duties. For if moral duties bear the marks of universality, immutability, and divine wisdom, it undeniably follows that they stem from an omniscient, omnipresent, and benevolent Lawgiver.

Concomitantly, moral duties are inextricably linked with human rights. This nexus between rights and duties is profoundly theological. If God, as Creator, endowed humanity with intrinsic dignity, then the duties we owe to one another are but the necessary responses to these God-given rights. Apologists must articulate how these duties serve as extensions of God's loving will, ensuring that every human being is treated in accordance with their inherent dignity.

At this juncture, it behooves us to weave the arguments for moral duties into the larger tapestry of theistic belief. Such duties, taken in their fullness, point towards an intelligent design and a purposeful Creator. The innate sense of duty perceived by humanity, argued with rigor, reflects the eternal moral order established by God. Hence, the believer finds a coherent and compelling narrative where moral duties are both justified and ennobled by the existence of a just and loving God.

Consider the duties of justice, charity, and the pursuit of the common good. These are not mere societal artifacts but divine commands. Justice, as the firm and constant will to give each their due, finds its higher justification in God's perfect justice. Charity, as the virtue that orders us to love our neighbors as ourselves, mirrors God's boundless love for every single soul. The common good, pursuing the flourishing of all, is a reflection of the communal aspect of the divine nature, calling us to see the interconnectedness ordained by the Creator.

Indeed, the apologetic task involves more than mere assertion; it requires rigorous demonstration of how these moral duties lead us toward theistic belief. Through logical coherence, historical continuity, and ethical necessity, we discern that moral duties are inherently theistic. They speak to an ordered reality where God is the ultimate author and sustainer of the moral law.

Additionally, the apologetic endeavor must address potential counterarguments. Critics might contend that moral duties can exist independent of divine origin, grounded merely in societal consensus or evolutionary benefit. However, such positions fall short. Societal consensus is mutable and capricious, while evolutionary explanations lack the prescriptive authority necessary for moral imperatives. Only a transcendent source, such as God, can provide the immutable and universal foundation for moral duties that transcend cultures, epochs, and individual preferences.

Moreover, the apologetic justification for moral duties must confront contemporary moral relativism. This worldview, which denies absolute moral truths, ultimately unravels under logical scrutiny. Without a divine anchor, moral duties are left afloat in a sea of subjective interpretations, devoid of absolute significance. Hence, the theistic framework provides the necessary foundation for objective moral duties, preserving their universality and binding nature.

The intertwining of rights and duties within the apologetic framework paints a harmonious picture of divine providence. The existence of these duties, infused with divine wisdom, affirms the presence of a moral lawgiver. Such an understanding not only strengthens faith but also provides a robust defense against the nihilistic inclinations of our age.

Thus, it stands that moral duties, far from being mere human constructs, reveal the depth of God's care and governance over His creation. Apologists must stress this divine-human connection, showcasing how these duties are consistent with the moral order presiding in the divine intellect. Recognizing these duties as divine commands calls us to a higher moral accountability and cements our understanding of God's sovereign role in moral legislation.

In closing, the apologetic justifications for moral duties beckon us to reflect deeply upon the divine origins of our moral obligations. This reflection not only affirms the existence of God but also enriches our understanding of the moral landscape upon which we tread. The divine source of our duties, intrinsically tied to human rights and dignity, offers profound implications for theology, ethics, and societal harmony.

As we ponder these lofty truths, may our hearts be ever guided by the light of reason and faith, leading us to embrace and fulfill our divine moral calling.

Chapter 5: Human Dignity as a Core Principle

In contemplating the essence of human dignity, we traverse the realms of the divine and the earthly, for it is an immutable truth inscribed within the heart of Catholic social doctrine. Human dignity is not merely an abstract concept but an intrinsic value bestowed upon each soul by the Creator, rendering every person a bearer of God's image. This inherent dignity demands an unwavering respect, transcending societal structures and human constructs. It calls for a recognition of each person's worth, not contingent upon accomplishments, social status, or material wealth, but rooted in their very existence. In intertwining the theological precepts with moral imperatives, we discern that human dignity is the cornerstone upon which both individual rights and social responsibilities rest. It compels us towards justice, urging that we advocate for the least among us, as every act of compassion and justice reflect the divine mandate. Thus, understanding human dignity becomes paramount in our pursuit of a just society, echoing the timeless wisdom that to honor human dignity is to honor the Creator Himself.

Theological Basis for Human Dignity

In the sacred tradition of the Roman Catholic Church, the concept of human dignity emerges not merely as an ethical principle but as a profound theological assertion. Indeed, human dignity stands at the very heart of Catholic Social Teaching, profoundly interwoven with the divine narrative of creation, redemption, and sanctification. To grasp the essence of this dignity, one must embark upon an exploration of the theological tenets that assert and protect it, delving deeply into sacred scripture, magisterial teachings, and the rich tapestry of theological reflection.

At the root of human dignity lies the foundational teaching that man is created in the image and likeness of God (Imago Dei), as stated in the Book of Genesis: "So God created man in his own image, in the image of God he created him; male and female he created them" (Genesis 1:27). This divine imprints upon humankind an inherent worth that transcends any societal or earthly estimation. The imago Dei connotes not merely a physical resemblance but a spiritual kinship that endows each person with an inalienable value and worth. Therefore, to respect human dignity is to recognize the divine image present in every individual.

Moreover, human dignity finds further affirmation in the mystery of the Incarnation. The Word became flesh and dwelt among us, thus sanctifying human nature through the person of Jesus Christ. This profound act of divine condescension underscores the immense value God places upon humanity. By assuming human form, Christ not only validates human worth but also redeems and elevates it. This theological truth illuminates the profound relationship between divinity and humanity, a relationship that demands recognition and reverence for each person's inherent dignity.

Beyond creation and redemption, the doctrine of sanctification provides another theological cornerstone for understanding human dignity. Through the sacraments and the work of the Holy Spirit, individuals are continually transformed into the likeness of Christ. This ongoing process of sanctification reaffirms the intrinsic worth of each person, who is constantly being molded and perfected as a reflection of God's glory. The call to holiness further emphasizes that human dignity is not a static attribute but a dynamic participation in divine grace.

Illuminating these theological insights, the magisterium of the Church has consistently affirmed the centrality of human dignity. Papal encyclicals, conciliar documents, and other magisterial teachings have underscored the inestimable worth of each person. For instance, in "Pacem in Terris," Pope John XXIII declares, "Each individual possesses a dignity which must be respected." Such ecclesiastical pronouncements reinforce the imperative to uphold human dignity in every sphere of life, extending from personal interactions to societal structures.

Theological reflection further elucidates human dignity through the virtue of charity. Rooted in the commandment to love one's neighbor as oneself, charity transcends mere benevolence and embodies an authentic recognition of the other's worth. This love originates in God's infinite love for humanity and calls each individual to respond in kind, respecting and honoring the dignity of others. By exercising charity, one acknowledges the divine image in the other and acts in accordance with the intrinsic value bestowed by God.

Furthermore, the principle of human dignity has significant ethical implications, grounded in the natural law tradition. Natural law, as articulated by the Angelic Doctor, Thomas Aquinas, asserts that moral truths are inscribed upon the human heart by the Creator. These truths, accessible through reason, direct individuals to act in ways that respect and promote human flourishing. The inviolability of human dignity underpins all moral obligations, guiding actions and policies that honor the intrinsic worth of every person.

In addition to its ethical dimensions, human dignity holds a unique place within the Church's social doctrine. Catholic Social Teaching, which addresses the array of social, economic, and political issues, begins with the recognition of human dignity as its foundational principle. Every encyclical and pastoral letter that speaks to social concerns, such as "Rerum Novarum" and "Gaudium et Spes," stresses that human dignity must be the basis upon which just societies are built. This teaching mandates that all social structures and policies respect the innate worth of the individual and promote the common good.

Beyond the philosophical and theological frameworks, the parables and teachings of Christ Himself reveal a profound commitment to human dignity. His ministry was replete with encounters that underscored the value of each person, especially those marginalized and oppressed. Christ's healing of the sick, His outreach to sinners, and His affirmation of the lowly attest to a divine recognition of human worth that transcends societal judgments and prejudices. In these actions, the Church finds a model for upholding human dignity irrespective of status, condition, or sinfulness.

Moreover, human dignity is inextricably linked to the concept of freedom, a theme richly explored in Catholic theological discourse. True freedom, as understood within the Church, is not merely the capacity to choose but the ability to choose the good. This freedom respects the dignity of the person and enables one to fulfill one's vocation. Divine grace assists in this endeavor, liberating individuals from the bondage of sin and enabling them to live in accordance with their true, dignified nature.

In conclusion, the theological basis for human dignity within Roman Catholicism is vast and profound, grounded in the doctrines of creation, incarnation, redemption, and sanctification. It is consistently affirmed by magisterial teachings and elaborated through ethical and social doctrines. At its core, the respect for human dignity flows from a recognition of the divine image in each person and the redemptive love of Christ. This understanding calls all believers to champion the inherent worth of all individuals, creating a society that honors God's creative, redemptive, and sanctifying work in every human life.

Implications for Social Justice

Human dignity, as a luminous beacon, illuminates the pathway to a just society. It forms the bedrock upon which the edifice of social justice stands. Rooted deeply within the sacred traditions of Catholic teaching, the inviolable nature of human dignity demands the respect and protection of every individual, irrespective of their station in life. This enduring principle calls forth the duty to recognize and uphold the inherent worth of each person, propelling forward the cause of justice in an ever-evolving tapestry of society.

In grappling with the notion of human dignity, we encounter a profound moral imperative. It beckons us to extend beyond mere acknowledgment and to strive for a practical realization of justice in all social spheres. The recognition of human dignity as fundamental invariably shapes policies, laws, and everyday interactions. This understanding invites all purveyors of justice—from theologians to judges, attorneys to politicians—to integrate these principles into the very fabric of their vocations.

When we deliberate upon human dignity, we must discern its implications across various facets of social life. For instance, in the realms of law and governance, human dignity necessitates the establishment of legal frameworks that safeguard the rights and freedoms of every individual. It compels the state to enact and enforce laws that protect the vulnerable, rectify inequalities, and promote the common good. Within the judiciary, it requires unbiased adjudication that honors the dignity of both the accuser and the accused.

In the sphere of economics and labor, the sanctity of human dignity demands fair wages, just working conditions, and the eradication of exploitative practices. A society that cherishes human dignity cannot tolerate the subjugation of workers or the perpetuation of poverty. It must ensure that each person is afforded the opportunity to contribute meaningfully to the commonweal, and that labor, as an expression of human creativity, is duly respected and rewarded.

Education, too, emerges as a critical arena where human dignity and social justice intersect. Every individual, imbued with innate worth, is entitled to the enrichment and empowerment that education provides. Social justice compels the availability of quality education for all, eschewing discrimination and fostering an environment where every learner can thrive. Education, in this light, becomes a powerful tool for achieving equity and uplifting marginalized communities.

Healthcare, a domain intrinsically tied to dignity, demands equitable access to medical services. The tenet of human dignity decries the neglect of the sick and the disenfranchised. It propels the call for compassionate, inclusive healthcare systems that treat every patient with respect and care. To ignore this is not only a medical oversight but a profound moral failing.

At its core, the principle of human dignity serves as a clarion call to action for all Catholic social teachings. In every social structure and institution, the infusion of this principle fosters a culture of respect, empathy, and compassion. It transcends mere rhetoric, requiring that political and social systems be continually reformed to echo its truths. Throughout history, this commitment has inspired movements, catalyzed reforms, and brought forth champions of justice who, fueled by the ethos of human dignity, have precipitated monumental changes.

Moreover, human dignity extends its reach to the ecclesial sphere, dictating the Church's role in societal transformation. It behooves the Church to be a prophetic voice, advocating for the rights and dignity of all, especially the marginalized and oppressed. It is a divine mandate that the Church, through its ministries and doctrines, acts as a moral compass, guiding society towards the realization of genuine justice.

The interconnectedness of human dignity and social justice also challenges the political sphere to reflect these values in policy-making and governance. Politicians and lawmakers are summoned to a higher ethos, one that transcends partisan interests and strives for the genuine welfare of all citizens. Human dignity, thus enshrined, becomes the yardstick against which all policies are measured, ensuring they contribute to the upholding of justice and equity.

It is through the prism of human dignity that we understand the profound implications for the rights of individuals in diverse situations. Whether considering the plight of refugees, the systemic discrimination faced by minorities, or the burgeoning crisis of poverty, human dignity compels us to engage with social justice issues holistically and empathetically. This core principle rejects any form of degradation or dehumanization and instead calls for advocacy, supportive interventions, and transformative actions that restore and affirm the dignity of every human life.

As we ponder the implications of human dignity for social justice, it becomes manifest that this principle embodies a universal call—one that reaches across boundaries and speaks to the shared humanity within us all. It resonates with the theological teachings of the Church and aligns seamlessly with the apologetic arguments for the existence of a just and benevolent Creator. In the tapestry of Catholic Social Teaching, the threads of human dignity and social justice are inextricably interwoven, forming an indomitable fabric that beckons us to craft a more just, compassionate, and humane world.

Chapter 6: The Common Good in Theology and Society

Verily, the discourse on the common good stands as a pillar within both theological contemplation and societal governance, intertwining the ethereal and the corporeal. The ecclesiastical doctrine proclaims that the common good transcends mere utilitarian aggregates, embodying instead a universal harmony envisioned by Divine Providence. This sacred principle beckons the faithful towards a collective pursuit, whereby individual rights find their fullest expression only through their subordination to communal welfare. In the realm of theology, the common good reveals a divine summons toward solidarity, advocating a confluence of love and justice as the cornerstone of societal order. It is the moral compass guiding legislators, judges, and every soul engaged in public service towards laws and actions that reflect divine wisdom, fostering an environment where human dignity is upheld, and the grace of God's kingdom can be mirrored on earth. Thus, the common good becomes not just an abstract ideal, but a tangible reality, binding society in a sacred covenant reflective of the divine order, and calling each of us to participate fervently in the unfolding of God's will within the human community.

Defining the Common Good

Delving ever deeper into the profundities of Catholic theology, we approach the pivotal notion of the common good. This concept, so vital and yet so widely misunderstood, serves as the cornerstone upon which the edifice of social justice stands. In a world teeming with individual interests and self-centered pursuits, the common good beckons us toward a more holistic vision, wherein the welfare of all is prioritized over the aggrandizement of a few.

Reflect, if you will, upon an ancient oak whose boughs shelter all manner of life. The strength of this venerable tree relies not upon its individual branches but upon the intricate interconnectedness of its entire form. Likewise, the common good draws its essence from the recognition that each soul, each human endeavor, is inextricably linked to the greater social fabric. The common good, then, is the summum bonum, or highest good, achievable only when society's structures and practices are oriented toward the flourishing of every member.

The common good transcends mere material wealth or temporal satisfaction. It encompasses the spiritual and moral well-being of individuals and communities. Within the rich tapestry of Catholic social teaching, the common good signifies a harmonious state where justice, peace, and righteousness are not distant ideals but lived realities. To chase the common good is to pursue a life wherein virtues blossom and vices wither under the gaze of divine providence.

St. Thomas Aquinas, a luminary in Catholic thought, viewed the common good as the ultimate aim of human society. For him, it is not a transient phenomenon but a reflection of the divine order itself. This celestial concord, mirrored imperfectly on earth, invites humanity to participate in God's eternal plan, making the alignment with the common good not merely a civic duty but a sacred vocation.

Yet, how do we define such an elusive and grandiose term? The common good can be encapsulated in three principal elements: respect for the person, social well-being and development, and peace. These elements are like the threefold chord described in Scripture, which is not easily broken and forms the unyielding foundation upon which the edifice of society must rest.

Respect for the person underscores the inherent dignity bestowed upon every human being by their Creator. Each individual, fashioned in the image and likeness of God, carries an inviolable sanctity that commands respect. In practice, this means safeguarding human rights, promoting moral growth, and ensuring that every person has the opportunity to contribute to society's moral and spiritual wealth.

Social well-being and development, the second element, urge us to forge pathways of growth that are inclusive and equitable. This extends beyond economic metrics or technological advancements to encompass the full spectrum of human potential. Education, healthcare, and a just economic order are not ends in themselves but means to foster an environment wherein every person can achieve their divinely ordained purpose.

The third element, peace, encapsulates more than mere absence of conflict. It represents a positive state of harmony and order, a reflection of God's shalom. True peace is birthed from justice, and justice, in turn, is the fruit of the common good. Thus, the pursuit of peace is synonymous with the pursuit of justice and the common good.

Governance and law, too, play crucial roles in nurturing the common good. Any legal framework or political system that seeks legitimacy must aspire to uphold these three elements. The authority of such systems is derived not from mere power but from their alignment with moral and divine laws. Hence, the rulers and judges, as stewards of justice, must ever bear the common good in their hearts, translating its lofty principles into concrete policies and fair judgments.

As the Apostle Paul exhorts in his epistle to the Corinthians, "Let all things be done decently and in order." This divine mandate extends to all strata of society but holds particular resonance for leaders and policymakers tasked with shepherding communities. The common good is neither static nor monolithic; it is dynamic, evolving to meet the needs and challenges of the times.

While philosophical treatises and theological dissertations may abound, the common good must ultimately be grasped through lived experience and communal striving. It calls for an ascetic dedication, akin to the monastic traditions that sought above all to glorify God through communal life. Herein lies the intersection of rights, responsibilities, and divine purpose, demanding that we look beyond the self and see in our neighbor the image of Christ.

Of course, the road to the common good is fraught with obstacles and misunderstandings. It is tempting to reduce the concept to a mere political or economic formula, but such reductionism betrays its transcendent nature. We must remain vigilant, lest we confuse the means for the ends, and in so doing, wander from the path of righteousness.

As modernity hurtles forward, awash in technological advancements and global interconnectedness, the common good remains a beacon, guiding us toward a society where the Kingdom of God is manifested more fully on earth. The pursuit requires humility, wisdom, and a fervent commitment to justice.

In conclusion, the common good is more than a theological abstraction or social ideal. It is a principle rooted in the very nature of God and mirrored in the essence of humanity. It invites us to a higher calling, urging us to transcend individualistic pursuits for the sake of a divine and just order. Let us, therefore, strive with all our might and sincerity to foster this common good, that we may reflect the Creator's intent and usher in a foretaste of the heavenly kingdom here on earth.

The Importance of the Common Good in Catholic Teaching

The principle of the common good occupies a place of paramount significance in the grand tapestry of Catholic teaching, anchoring myriad doctrines that aim to weave a social fabric in harmonious alignment with divine ordinances. In essence, the common good bespeaks an intrinsic social order wherein the flourishing of each individual is conjoined with the welfare of the entire community. This concept finds its roots in both natural law and divine revelation, compelling believers to transcend mere individualism in pursuit of a collective human flourishing.

Central to Catholic social teaching is the idea that the common good forms the bedrock upon which all ethical imperatives and societal laws are constructed. The encyclicals and pastoral letters of the Church's magisterium often reiterate that individuals are bound by a moral duty to seek the common good, not as an abstract ideal, but as a lived reality manifest in societal structures and relationships. This principle asserts that personal fulfillment can only be authentically realized when one simultaneously works towards the alleviation of communal suffering and promotion of collective well-being.

St. Thomas Aquinas, a luminary in Catholic theological thought, expounded that the common good is essentially the good proper to, and attainable only by, the community, yet is predicated upon the moral actions of individuals. Thus, the pursuit of the common good necessitates a reciprocal relationship between personal virtue and communal responsibility. This theological perspective underscores the Church's holistic understanding of human existence, which amalgamates individual and societal dimensions into an inseparable unity.

Yet, what constitutes the common good? It transcends mere material prosperity and extends to the immaterial realms of justice, peace, and honest stewardship of creation. The common good mandates that all members of society possess access to basic human rights such as food, shelter, education, and healthcare. However, it also entails the moral and spiritual betterment of society, where virtues such as charity, prudence, and justice are inculcated and exemplified.

The common good, in its fullest sense, is inextricably linked to the concept of human dignity. Catholic teaching posits that every human being, created in the image and likeness of God, possesses inherent worth. Therefore, the pursuit of the common good involves the recognition and respect of this dignity in every social endeavor. This principle challenges any socio-political system or economic model that marginalizes or exploits individuals, advocating instead for systems that elevate and dignify each person within the collective whole.

In practical terms, the importance of the common good manifests itself in the Church's social doctrine, which calls for just governance, equitable distribution of resources, and the fostering of environments where human potential can be fully realized. The Church teaches that societal policies and laws must prioritize the common good over individual gain, balancing private rights with public responsibilities. This aligns with the Church's advocacy for social justice, wherein the emphasis is laid upon rectifying injustices that hinder the realization of the common good.

Moreover, the essence of the common good calls upon believers to engage actively in social and political life. As stewards of creation and co-creators in God's salvific plan, Catholics are urged to participate in civil discourse, vote conscientiously, and advocate for policies that reflect the moral teachings of the Church. This civic engagement is not merely a right but a duty, grounded in the moral imperative to seek the communal welfare over individualistic pursuits.

Pope John XXIII elucidated this doctrine in his encyclical *Mater et Magistra*, where he emphasized the role of community and solidarity in the pursuit of the common good. He stressed that an authentic social order must be animated by a spirit of mutual aid and cooperation, echoing the Gospel's call to love one's neighbor. This papal teaching aligns with the broader Catholic understanding that the common good is not a static end but a dynamic process, continually shaped by human actions and relationships.

The common good also finds profound resonance in the teachings of the Second Vatican Council, particularly in the document *Gaudium et Spes*. Here, the Council Fathers delineated that the Church's mission is intimately connected with the welfare of the human family, calling upon all men of good will to collaborate in the construction of a just society. The Council articulated that the common good encompasses not only the social and economic dimensions but also the moral and spiritual realms, necessitating a holistic approach to human development.

Furthermore, the pursuit of the common good necessitates a preferential option for the poor and vulnerable. Catholic teaching asserts that true justice involves prioritizing the needs of the marginalized, ensuring that societal resources and opportunities are allocated in a manner that uplifts those most in need. This principle is a clarion call to solidarity, urging believers to commit their lives to the service of others, particularly those who are often forgotten or oppressed.

The common good also involves fostering a culture of peace. Catholic teaching emphasizes that peace is not merely the absence of conflict but the presence of justice and charity. The common good thus requires proactive efforts to resolve conflicts, promote understanding, and build societies rooted in mutual respect and love. This necessitates an unwavering commitment to nonviolence, reconciliation, and the construction of social structures that deter injustice and promote harmony.

Importantly, the Church's teaching on the common good also extends to ecological concerns. The call to care for creation is an integral aspect of seeking the common good, as environmental degradation disproportionately affects the poor and undermines the collective well-being. The Church urges responsible stewardship of the earth, advocating for sustainable practices that preserve the integrity of creation for future generations. This ecological dimension of the common good aligns with the broader call to justice and respect for all life.

In summation, the importance of the common good in Catholic teaching cannot be overstated. It serves as a guiding star, illuminating the path towards a just and harmonious society where every individual's dignity is respected, and all are afforded the opportunity to thrive. In a world often fractured by division and self-interest, the Church's teaching on the common good offers a compelling vision of unity, justice, and love, grounded in divine wisdom and human solidarity.

Chapter 7: Natural Law and Moral Order

As we delve into the profound interplay between Natural Law and Moral Order, we find ourselves amidst the very bedrock of theological and philosophical inquiry that has resonated through the corridors of time, from St. Augustine to the present day. Natural Law, as conceived in the Catholic tradition, is not merely a set of ethical guidelines but the divine orchestration written into the very fabric of human existence, governing all with immutable precision. It serves as the compass of our moral conscience, guiding individuals to discern right from wrong by the light of inherent reason and divine inspiration. Inextricably linked to this concept is the Moral Order, which manifests the practical applications of Natural Law in our societal constructs. Through the harmonious alignment of human law with divine precepts, justice finds its lifeblood, birthing an environment where human rights are not just acknowledged but revered as sacred. Such an integration compels us to navigate our civic duties and moral responsibilities with unwavering fidelity, reflecting the divine symphony in our terrestrial realm.

The Concept of Natural Law

In the grand tapestry of moral reasoning, the notion of Natural Law weaves its threads with sublime intricacy, casting light upon the inherent principles imbued within the cosmos by the Divine Creator. Anchored in the bedrock of Catholic theology, Natural Law forms the eternal bedrock upon which human rights and moral imperatives are founded. Its resonance extends beyond mere mortal deliberations, harkening to an immutable, universal order discernible through reason and intellect.

Natural Law, in its essence, is an expression of God's eternal will inscribed within the very fabric of creation. Unlike positive laws contrived by human legislatures, this Divine ordinance is unchanging and universal, transcending the vicissitudes of time and culture. It beckons to the rational soul, calling forth an acknowledgment of the Good, the True, and the Just.

This Divine ordinance does not speak in the cacophony of human tongues but resonates in the silent chambers of conscience. It is therein that one perceives the echo of eternal truths, guiding the moral compass steadfastly. The soul, in its pursuit of virtue, aligns with the immutable precepts of justice, fortitude, temperance, and prudence, all of which derive from this celestial law.

Famed theologians and philosophers, within the august tradition of the Church, have articulated the alignment of human nature with these transcendent principles. Thomas Aquinas, for instance, illuminates the relationship between divine wisdom and human reason. In his "Summa Theologica," Aquinas posits that Natural Law is nothing other than the rational creature's participation in the eternal law, a reflection of God's own reason.

According to Aquinas, this participation is not passive; it demands the rigorous application of reason to discern the proper course of action in every circumstance. Human beings, endowed with intellect and free will, are called upon to act in accordance with these indelible truths, ensuring that their deeds are consonant with the higher order of justice and charity.

The role Natural Law plays within moral theology cannot be overstated. It forms the substratum upon which the edifice of moral responsibility is constructed. From it flow the fundamental rights and obligations that bind humanity in a universal fraternity. It posits that every human being, by virtue of their rational nature, is entitled to respect and dignity.

Thus do human laws find their legitimacy in their conformity to this higher law. When a statute runs contrary to the principles of Natural Law, it is deemed unjust, lacking in moral authority. As St. Augustine so succinctly stated, "An unjust law is no law at all."

Yet, it must be noted, the discernment of Natural Law is not bereft of challenges. Human intellect, clouded by sin and concupiscence, may falter in apprehending these divine truths. Thus does the Church, through her magisterium, guide the faithful in understanding and applying these principles in the temporal realm.

The role of Natural Law extends into diverse domains of human existence. It informs ethical deliberations in matters of life, justice, governance, and interpersonal relations. It establishes the framework through which human acts are evaluated and moral judgments pronounced.

In the sphere of social justice, the precepts of Natural Law affirm the intrinsic worth of every individual. Rights to life, liberty, and the pursuit of happiness are not mere social constructs but tangible expressions of this divine ordinance. Social institutions, therefore, are tasked with upholding these rights, fostering an environment in which human dignity and the common good are paramount.

Moreover, Natural Law serves as a touchstone for human laws, ensuring that they are grounded in an objective moral order. Legislators and judges are called upon to craft and interpret laws in a manner that upholds these transcendent truths. Failure to do so results in a dissonance that reverberates through the social fabric, leading to injustice and societal discord.

The eloquence of Natural Law lies in its simplicity and universality, yet its application requires profound wisdom and prudence. In a world rife with moral relativism and ethical ambiguity, it stands as a beacon of clarity and moral certitude. It reminds humanity of its higher calling, urging a return to the fundamentals of virtue and the embrace of the common good.

In the tapestry of life, the concept of Natural Law is a golden thread, uniting the temporal with the eternal. It beckons each soul to strive for the good, the true, and the just, forging a path that leads to the ultimate telos ordained by Divine Providence. As such, it is not merely a philosophical construct but a lived reality, imbibing every action and decision with profound significance.

It is incumbent upon all, therefore, to heed this celestial injunction, to align one's will with the divine precepts, and to contribute to the establishment of a moral order that reflects the harmony of the heavens. In doing so, one participates in the divine orchestration of the cosmos, fulfilling the higher purpose for which humanity was created.

The majesty of Natural Law endures, a testament to the eternal wisdom of our Creator and a guiding light for all who seek to walk in the way of righteousness. May this sublime truth continue to inspire and illuminate, drawing countless souls to the embrace of divine justice and eternal peace.

Natural Law and Its Relation to Human Rights

In the grand tapestry of Divine ordinance and moral order, wherein the threads of existence intertwine with the celestial laws, the concept of Natural Law emerges as a beacon illuminating the inherent dignity of humanity. Within the sacred precincts of Catholic thought, Natural Law is not merely an abstract principle but a profound existential reality that underscores the moral architecture of the universe. It is within this hallowed framework that we discern the inextricable relation between Natural Law and Human Rights.

Natural Law, as articulated through the wisdom of ages, posits that there exists an inherent order established by the Creator, which governs all creation. This order is not imposed arbitrarily; rather, it is woven into the very fabric of our being. It is a reflection of the divine reason and a testament to the inherent rationality of the divine plan. Human beings, fashioned in the imago Dei, or the image of God, are endowed with the capacity to apprehend this Natural Law through the light of reason. Hence, the pursuit of truth and justice cannot be extricated from the recognition of this divinely instituted order.

The notion of Human Rights springs forth from this wellspring of Natural Law. Indeed, the very concept of rights owes its genesis to the understanding that certain moral standards are intrinsic to human nature. These standards, immutable and perpetual, stem from the purpose for which humanity was created. The recognition of human dignity, therefore, becomes the cornerstone upon which the edifice of human rights is constructed. By virtue of this dignity, every person is entitled to fundamental rights, such as the right to life, liberty, and the pursuit of happiness.

Inextricably linked to the Natural Law is the concept of justice, which serves as its sentinel. Justice demands that rights are not merely recognized but respected and safeguarded. It is through the lens of Natural Law that judges, lawmakers, and those entrusted with the stewardship of society are called to discern the rightful claims of individuals and communities. Therefore, the preservation of human rights becomes not only a legal obligation but a moral imperative, ordained by the Creator and inscribed within the human heart.

In this grand scheme, it is essential to recognize that the rights accorded to individuals are intertwined with corresponding responsibilities. Rights and responsibilities are two sides of the same moral coin, and no right can exist detached from its correlative duty. The Natural Law elucidates this profound truth, imparting the wisdom that the exercise of rights must always harmonize with the common good. To act otherwise would be to contradict the very essence of our nature and the divine order that sustains it.

The Church, through its magisterium, has consistently upheld the principles of Natural Law as foundational to its social teaching. Documents like "Rerum Novarum" and "Pacem in Terris" articulate the Church's commitment to the promotion of human rights grounded in Natural Law. The teachings assert that genuine social justice can only be achieved when human rights are recognized as divinely ordained, in alignment with the Natural Law that dictates our moral duties.

Theologians and philosophers have long contended that the articulation of human rights apart from Natural Law leads to a relativistic and fragmented moral order. When rights are untethered from the objective moral order, they become vulnerable to the whims of societal trends and the caprices of power. Thus, the safeguarding of human rights necessitates a steadfast adherence to Natural Law, an unwavering commitment to the guiding principles of divine wisdom.

Moreover, politicians, judges, and attorneys, called to serve the public good, must ground their actions and decisions in the moral truths revealed by Natural Law. The establishment of just laws and equitable policies rests upon the recognition that human rights are not arbitrary constructs but reflections of the Divine Will. In this light, the pursuit of justice becomes a sacred duty, an act of participating in the divine governance of the world.

Natural Law and its connection to human rights also beckon to the conscience of every individual. It demands a personal commitment to the moral order, urging each person to uphold and defend the rights of others as fervently as one's own. The call to love one's neighbor, enshrined in the Gospel, resonates with the principles of Natural Law, compelling a deep respect for the dignity and rights of others.

In conclusion, the profound relation between Natural Law and human rights elucidates the path to authentic social justice. By recognizing and embracing the divinely instituted moral order, we affirm the inherent dignity of every person and commit to the protection of their rights. The teachings of the Church, the wisdom of the ages, and the call to moral integrity all converge in this enduring truth: that the Natural Law is the fount from which the rights of humanity flow, guiding us towards the realization of a just and harmonious society.

Chapter 8: Scriptural Basis for Social Justice

As we traverse the annals of Holy Scripture, mandates for justice resound with divine authority. The Old Testament prophet Micah proclaims, "To act justly and to love mercy and to walk humbly with your God," a clarion call resonating through the corridors of time, commanding believers towards justice and compassion. The New Testament fortifies this ethos, with Jesus' parable of the Good Samaritan elevating love for neighbor as bedrock for righteous living. Paul's letters, too, exhort the faithful to bear one another's burdens, enshrining solidarity as a cardinal virtue. Hence, the sacred texts, both ancient and apostolic, illumine a path where social justice intertwines with God's commandments, weaving a moral tapestry that beckons the faithful toward equitable stewardship and ceaseless advocacy for the downtrodden. Thus, through the scriptural lens, justice transcends mere obligation, manifesting as a divine imperative, a testament to God's enduring call for a just and compassionate society.

Key Biblical Passages on Justice

The sacred scriptures, in their ageless wisdom, offer profound insights into the essence of justice, intertwined with divine grace and human responsibility. Yea, consider the venerable Deuteronomy 16:20, where it is written: "Justice, justice shalt thou pursue, that thou mayest live, and inherit the land which the Lord thy God giveth thee." In these hallowed words, the dual repetition of 'justice' signifies not mere legality but a deep, unwavering commitment to moral righteousness.

Similarly, the prophet Micah enjoins: "He hath shewed thee, O man, what is good; and what doth the Lord require of thee, but to do justly, and to love mercy, and to walk humbly with thy God?" (Micah 6:8). This tripartite exhortation captures the essence of divine justice, mercy, and humility, entwining them as the beacon of righteous living for both the individual and society.

Transitioning to the Psalms, one finds the justice of the Lord proclaimed in poetic grandeur. Psalm 82:3-4 exhorts: "Defend the poor and fatherless: do justice to the afflicted and needy. Deliver the poor and needy: rid them out of the hand of the wicked." This directive mandates active intervention for the downtrodden and affirms the intrinsic worth of every human soul, mirroring the divine image.

The Proverbs further elucidate justice with pragmatic wisdom. Proverbs 21:15 declares, "It is joy to the just to do judgment: but destruction shall be to the workers of iniquity." Here, the pleasure derived from rightful judgment is juxtaposed starkly against the ruin awaiting evildoers, emphasizing the dual paths of righteousness and wickedness.

In the New Testament, Christ's parables and teachings offer a sublime standard for justice. The Sermon on the Mount, particularly, in Matthew 5-7, brims with ethical precepts that call for justice tempered by mercy. "Blessed are they which do hunger and thirst after righteousness: for they shall be filled" (Matthew 5:6) is a clarion call, urging relentless pursuit of justice.

Moreover, in Matthew 25:35-40, our Lord presents the parable of the sheep and the goats, where he avers, "For I was an hungred, and ye gave me meat: I was thirsty, and ye gave me drink: I was a stranger, and ye took me in." This parable underscores the requisite of aiding the vulnerable as a measure of divine justice, binding the love of neighbor to the love of God.

Furthermore, the epistles of St. Paul offer theological profundities on justice. In Romans 12:19, the Apostle exhorts: "Dearly beloved, avenge not yourselves, but rather give place unto wrath: for it is written, Vengeance is mine; I will repay, saith the Lord." This passage calls for patience and faith in divine justice, eschewing personal retribution.

James the Just, in his epistle, proclaims: "Pure religion and undefiled before God and the Father is this, To visit the fatherless and widows in their affliction, and to keep himself unspotted from the world" (James 1:27). Thus, true piety is manifest in acts of justice and mercy toward the afflicted, a creed deeply embedded in Catholic social teaching.

Additionally, the imperative for communal justice resonates in the Acts of the Apostles. Acts 4:32-35 recounts the early Christian community, where "neither was there any among them that lacked: for as many as were possessors of lands or houses sold them, and brought the prices of the things that were sold, And laid them down at the apostles' feet: and distribution was made unto every man according as he had need." This portrayal of shared resources exemplifies just stewardship and care for the collective well-being.

Thus, throughout both the Old and New Testaments, the divine call to justice is unambiguous and commanding. From the ancient prophets to the teachings of Christ and the Apostles, the Scriptures beckon us to act justly, love mercy, and walk humbly with God. Indeed, these passages provide not merely historical insight but a living testament, guiding the faithful toward achieving a just and equitable society, grounded in the eternal principles of divine justice.

New Testament Teachings on Social Responsibility

The teachings of the New Testament, rich and manifold, bring forth an ethos that champions social responsibility with a vigor both revelatory and transformative. Christ's ministry, as captured in the Gospels, lays a foundation for believers to adhere to principles of justice, mercy, and service to others. The words and deeds of Jesus Christ, along with the exhortations of apostles such as Paul and James, constitute a vibrant tapestry that weaves the fabric of social responsibility deeply into the believer's life.

One cannot begin any exposition of New Testament teachings on this topic without first considering the Parable of the Good Samaritan (Luke 10:25-37). This parable illuminates Christ's command to love our neighbors as ourselves, transcending cultural and ethnic boundaries that were so rigidly defined in His time. The Samaritan's actions exemplify the call to act with compassion and mercy, challenging societal prejudices and urging a radical departure from apathy and indifference.

Moreover, in the Gospel according to Matthew, the Sermon on the Mount (Matthew 5-7) outlines numerous precepts that are as relevant today as they were two millennia ago. Through the Beatitudes, Christ blesses those who seek righteousness, mercy, and peacemaking. "Blessed are the peacemakers," He declares, for they shall be called the children of God (Matthew 5:9). This beatitude, among others, underscores the commitment required to pursue social harmony and justice, extending beyond mere tolerance to active reconciliation and peace.

The New Testament further details social responsibilities through the words of the apostle Paul, particularly in his letters to various early Christian communities. In his Epistle to the Romans, Paul emphatically states, "Let love be genuine; hate what is evil, hold fast to what is good; love one another with mutual affection; outdo one another in showing honor" (Romans 12:9-10). Here, Paul calls the faithful to authentic love and communal respect, fostering an environment where justice and altruism thrive, reinforcing the communal aspect of ethical living wherein each person bears a duty to contribute to the common good.

Paul continues this exhortation in his Epistle to the Galatians, wherein he writes, "Bear one another's burdens, and in this way you will fulfill the law of Christ" (Galatians 6:2). This passage emphasizes the importance of solidarity, urging believers to support one another through trials and tribulations. By bearing the burdens of others, Christians engage in a profound act of love that echoes Christ's own sacrifice, embodying the social responsibility inherent in the New Testament teachings.

Another vital aspect of social responsibility is elucidated in the Epistle of James, which famously declares, "Faith without works is dead" (James 2:26). This admonition serves as a clarion call for an active faith, one that manifests through tangible acts of justice and mercy. The notion that belief, deprived of action, is insubstantial, compels Christians to engage in charitable works, advocating for the oppressed and fostering a more equitable society.

Additionally, the Acts of the Apostles provides a historical account of the early Christian community, highlighting the communal life they led. The believers, we read, "had all things in common" and "distributed to each as any had need" (Acts 2:44-45). This early communalism reflects an ideal of economic justice and mutual support, establishing a precedent for future generations to address social disparities and practice distributive justice.

An essential teaching of Jesus that further expounds on social responsibility is found in Matthew 25:31-46, where He speaks of the Final Judgment. In this passage, Christ identifies with the least among us, stating that acts of kindness toward the hungry, the thirsty, the stranger, the naked, the sick, and the imprisoned are acts done unto Him. "Truly I tell you, just as you did it to one of the least of these who are members of my family, you did it to me" (Matthew 25:40). This identification underscores a profound theological and ethical directive to care for the marginalized and the vulnerable, thereby fulfilling our social responsibilities.

In essence, New Testament teachings on social responsibility are a call to live out the principles of love, mercy, justice, and service. These teachings enjoin Christians to look beyond their own needs and desires, to consider the well-being of others, and to foster a community where the dignity of every person is respected and upheld. Through acts of charity, advocacy for justice, and a communal life rooted in love and service, believers are called to embody the values of the Kingdom of God in their daily lives.

Thus, the New Testament's instruction on social responsibility is not mere moralizing but a radical invitation to partake in the transformative work of building a just and compassionate society. It calls for a continual conversion of heart, prompting believers to be vigilant in acts of justice and mercy, and to constantly seek ways to alleviate the suffering of others. In doing so, Christians bear witness to the Gospel's life-affirming power and participate in the redemptive mission of Christ, who came not to be served, but to serve.

Chapter 9: The Role of Grace and Free Will

Connecting the celestial strings between grace and free will unveils a tapestry of divine interaction and moral autonomy, each strand essential in Catholic theology. Grace, the unmerited favor bestowed by the Almighty, acts as a catalyst to kindle the human soul towards acts of virtue and charity. Simultaneously, free will stands as the cornerstone of human moral agency, granting the power to choose righteousness or transgression. This delicate balance emphasizes not the subjugation of human will by divine omnipotence, but rather a harmonious dance where grace enables and free will chooses. Thus, grace and free will, though seemingly disparate elements, merge to frame a cohesive understanding of ethical responsibility and divine indispensability, heralding a journey toward spiritual fulfillment and social justice.

Theological Perspectives on Grace

In the grand tapestry of Catholic theology, the concept of grace is paramount and finds itself intricately woven into the complexities of human existence and divine intervention. For the learned theologian, as well as the devout jurist and legislator, an understanding of grace is indispensable when exploring the interplay between faith and morality.

To fathom the depths of grace, one must travel through a labyrinth of divine favor, wherein grace is seen as an unmerited and gratuitous gift bestowed by God upon man. The ecclesiastical tradition, deeply seeded in the writings of the Church Fathers, illuminates grace as the lifeblood of spiritual regeneration and sanctification. Herein, grace is not merely a passive endowment but an active force, invigorating the soul to pursue righteousness and to fulfill one's moral obligations.

Saint Augustine delineates grace as the fundamental means by which the human will is turned toward the good. In his epistles, one encounters a profound explication of the dynamic relationship between divine grace and free will. Augustine posits that it is by grace that the human heart is softened and predisposed to receive divine truths. Thus, the human capacity for moral action and ethical behavior is inexorably linked to this divine influence.

Similarly, Thomas Aquinas, in his *Summa Theologica*, amplifies the role of grace within the paradigm of human agency. Aquinas opines that grace perfects nature; it does not destroy it. The human intellect and will, though capable of discerning good, are elevated and perfected by grace. This elevates the human person to participate in the divine life. Aquinas elucidates that grace operates in both a prevenient manner, preparing the soul for the reception of God's mercy, and a cooperative manner, where the human will synergizes with divine grace.

The Magisterium, in its sagacity, has expounded upon grace in a manner that resounds with both the spiritual and temporal spheres. The Council of Trent, convened amidst the throes of the Reformation, dogmatically declared that justification is accomplished by divine grace through faith, independent of human merits. This pronounced the universality and efficacy of grace, asserting its indispensability in the salvific process.

Moreover, in contemporary theological discourse, grace is perceived through a prism that acknowledges the multifaceted nature of human challenges and societal inequities. Liberation theologians, for instance, conceive grace as an impetus for social transformation and justice. Here, grace transcends personal sanctification and extends to the liberation of the oppressed and the establishment of just societal structures.

Yet, the convergence of grace and free will natural unfolds a dialectic that has both confounded and inspired the faithful. Amidst this dialectic, one must contemplate the inherent tension between divine predestination and human autonomy. This tension is not just theological but philosophically rich, invoking the eternal questions of fate, freedom, and moral responsibility.

Jansenism, emerging in the 17th century, accentuated divine predestination to the extent of diminishing human free will, thereby inciting vehement debate and eventual repudiation by the Church. This sect's rigoristic interpretation underscored the necessity for a balanced recognition of both divine grace and human freedom.

Conversely, contemporary Catholic thought, though enriched by the Church's magisterial teachings, continually engages with this dialectic. The Second Vatican Council's pastoral constitution, *Gaudium et Spes*, succinctly asserts the sanctity of human freedom while unreservedly acknowledging the primacy of divine grace. This text, pervasive in its ecumenism, invites the faithful to discern one's role in God's salvific plan through the conscientious exercise of free will enlightened by grace.

In examining these theological perspectives, it becomes imperative to recognize that grace inexorably calls the believer to a life of moral excellence and justice. Enkindled by grace, the human person finds the fortitude to confront ethical dilemmas and advocates for a just social order.

Thus, the vocation of the jurist, the statesman, or the theologian is not merely an exercise in professional or intellectual rigor but a response to the divine call—an affirmation of the gift of grace that propels one to seek the common good, to defend human dignity, and to uphold the moral fabric of society.

Ultimately, the theological perspectives on grace offer a profound insight into the nature of divine-human interaction. By embracing these perspectives, one is better equipped to navigate the moral imperatives of rights and responsibilities, thereby contributing to the broader discourse on social justice and the existential quest for God. Grace, as both a gift and a call, remains at the heart of this divine-human symphony, harmonizing the individual's journey with the incessant pursuit of the divine will and the realization of a just and compassionate society.

Free Will and its Ethical Implications

The realm of free will, entwined with its profound ethical implications, holds an esteemed place in theological discourse, in particular within the purviews of Catholic doctrine. The dance between divine grace and human autonomy forms a foundational cornerstone, revealing not merely the essence of human moral agency but also the scope of our responsibilities and the magnificence of divine providence. The liberty to choose between good and ill, a gift bestowed upon humanity, renders the act of will an exercise in moral seriousness and spiritual gravitas.

The very notion of free will presupposes a capacity for deliberate consent or dissent, a sovereignty over one's actions that echoes the imago Dei—the image of God—in mankind. This faculty of self-determination is a testament to our distinct place within the created order, affirming that moral actions are not mere happenstances but ethical endeavors aimed at the virtuous or the vile. From this perspective, the ability to choose imparts upon us an ethical burden, a weighty responsibility to align our choices with the objective good, an ideal that finds its ultimate fulfillment in divine law and the teachings of the Church.

Consider the ethical ramifications of free will in the context of social justice, a core tenet of Catholic teaching. Society's moral structure fundamentally relies upon individuals exercising their free will in a manner that upholds justice, protects human dignity, and fosters the common good. A just society is not an accidental aggregation of fortuitous events but the product of intentional and virtuous acts by its members. Each individual's decision to act justly or unjustly has cascading effects, influencing the broader social fabric and either contributing to or detracting from the collective moral order.

The exercise of free will, thus, is seen as an ethical undertaking with both personal and societal dimensions. When one's choices are grounded in the pursuit of the good, they affirm and reinforce the principles of Catholic social teaching. Conversely, choices that deviate from this path undercut these principles and contribute to a culture of ethical relativism or moral decay. Free will, wielded responsibly, propels humanity toward its highest calling, while its misuse heralds ethical and spiritual decline.

It is crucial to consider the theological interplay between grace and free will. The Catholic tradition asserts that grace perfects nature. Divine assistance does not obliterate human freedom but elevates it, enabling a higher adherence to the good. While God's grace is indispensable for salvation and sanctity, it harmonizes with human free will, allowing individuals to freely cooperate with divine aid. This cooperation informs and enriches ethical decision-making, transcending mere natural capabilities and aligning with supernatural virtues.

Yet, herein lies a paradox that has intrigued theologians and philosophers alike: if divine grace influences human will, does it not compromise human freedom? To untangle this conundrum, one must delve deeper into the doctrine of grace. Far from coercing or diminishing our autonomy, grace liberates the will from the bondage of sin, enhancing its capacity to choose the good. St. Augustine famously posited that true freedom is found in pursuing righteousness, a freedom realized through the transformative power of grace.

Sacred Scripture sheds light on this complex relationship. The Apostle Paul's epistles often emphasize that believers are "co-workers" with God, suggesting a synergistic model where human and divine action intersect. The interplay between grace and free will is thus depicted as a cooperative endeavor, each respecting the operations of the other. This synergy compels us to consider ethical behavior not as a series of autonomous decisions, but as choices made within the context of divine influence and moral responsibility.

Additionally, ethical implications radiate from the acknowledgment that free will is not an isolated attribute but one intrinsically linked to moral and spiritual development. The cultivation of virtues—prudence, justice, fortitude, and temperance—necessitates the active engagement of free will. The will must consistently choose virtuous actions, participating in the gradual shaping of a moral character aligned with divine will and reflective of sanctity. Such a process underscores the formative role of free will in ethical life, affirming that our moral aspirations and actualities are deeply intertwined.

Further complicating the ethical landscape is the reality of moral evil, a perplexing manifestation of free will's misuse. The problem of evil, both moral and natural, challenges our understanding of free will and divine goodness. From an ethical standpoint, the existence of moral evil illustrates the perilous potential of free will when divorced from divine and moral guidance. It reveals the dark consequences of choices that repudiate the good, spotlighting the profound need for a moral compass anchored in divine wisdom and ecclesiastical teaching.

The ethical implications of free will extend to societal constructs, where systems of justice hinge on the premise of individual accountability. In a court of law, for instance, the notion of criminal responsibility presupposes that the individual had the free will to choose between lawful and unlawful actions. Ethical and legal systems alike rely on the concept of free will to administer justice fairly and proportionately, underscoring the vital role of personal agency in societal order.

Moreover, in political and legal spheres, free will informs democratic principles and human rights. The capacity for self-governance, rooted in free will, is a bedrock principle of democratic institutions that champion the moral and political autonomy of individuals. These institutions aim to create an environment where free will can be exercised responsibly and ethically, fostering a society where rights and responsibilities are balanced and justice is pursued as a collective ideal.

Justice, in this context, is not merely a juridical concept but a moral compass guiding collective and individual behavior toward the common good. Ensuring social justice involves a conscientious application of free will toward creating equitable structures that reflect divine justice and uphold human dignity. The responsible exercise of free will by leaders, lawmakers, and citizens alike is indispensable in shaping policies that promote fairness, protect rights, and fulfill social responsibilities.

In summation, free will and its ethical implications form a pivotal dialogue within Catholic teaching, permeating various facets of personal and communal life. It reveals the magnitude of human responsibility, the transcendent support of divine grace, and the moral imperative to align human choices with the ultimate good. Our moral agency, therefore, serves as both a gift and a task, inviting us to cooperate with divine grace in an ongoing pursuit of justice, dignity, and the common good.

Chapter 10: Historical Perspectives on Social Justice

In tracing the history of Social Justice, one discovers an intricate tapestry woven through the annals of Church doctrine and praxis. From the early exhortations of Church Fathers, who saw the imago Dei in every soul and therefore championed the poor and marginalized, to the medieval scholastics, who rigorously articulated the relationship between charity and justice, Social Justice has evolved with profound theological underpinnings. The Medieval period, marked by Thomas Aquinas' synthesis of Aristotelian philosophy with Christian doctrine, gave birth to an enduring moral framework that emphasized both individual rights and communal responsibilities. As ecclesiastical thought progressed, so did its application to societal constructs, making Social Justice a transcendental principle embedded within both ethical and social dimensions of Catholic teaching. Such historical developments have continuously illuminated the Church's unwavering commitment to justice, not merely as a secular ideal, but as a sacred responsibility born from divine command.

Early Church Teachings

The roots of social justice within the framework of the Catholic Church can be traced to the nascent years of Christianity. From the outset, the early Church Fathers, through their profound spiritual and theological insights, laid the foundation for a comprehensive and enduring notion of justice. These seminal teachings were woven into the very fabric of the early Christian community, cementing a collective identity that deeply valued the principles of equity and righteousness.

In the first centuries following the death and resurrection of Christ, the Apostolic Fathers such as St. Clement of Rome, St. Ignatius of Antioch, and St. Polycarp gave voice to the teachings of Jesus through their epistles and exhortations. Their writings reveal a tenet of faith that emphasizes the harmony of belief and practice. To live as a Christian was not solely about inward piety but also about outward manifestations of love and charity. The primitive Church saw the dual dimensions of justice—legal and social—as indispensable to the Christian way of life, aspiring to mirror the divine justice of God within human society.

Furthermore, the Didache, known as "The Teaching of the Twelve Apostles," offers a comprehensive view of early Christian moral directives. Distinguished by its practical advice on communal living and liturgical practice, the Didache underscores the importance of distributive justice. It insists on the fair allocation of resources and the imperative to care for the less fortunate, reflecting an early ecclesiastical commitment to social justice. The Didache urges believers to share their wealth, avoid partiality, and uphold the dignity of all members within the Christian community.

In the writings of the Church Fathers, one finds a recurring theme: the assertion that wealth and resources are given by God for the benefit of all. St. John Chrysostom, renowned for his eloquence and deep theological insights, staunchly advocated for the care of the poor. He viewed the affluent as stewards, rather than owners, of their riches and fervently spoke against idleness and excessive luxury. His homilies vibrantly echo the message that neglecting the destitute is tantamount to neglecting Christ Himself, a poignant reminder of Jesus' parable concerning the sheep and the goats.

Similarly, St. Basil the Great, whose sermons and letters were steeped in Christian socialism, propagates another vital aspect of social justice—the redistribution of wealth. He decried the hoarding of goods while others languished in poverty and championed the establishment of hospitals and charitable institutions. To him, true piety was inseparable from generativity and service to the vulnerable. His influential work "Homilies on the Psalms" is particularly notable for its rigorous theological exposition on the moral obligations of the rich towards the poor.

Alongside Basil, his contemporary St. Gregory of Nyssa made substantial contributions to the theological discourse on social justice. Gregory's anthropological understanding of humanity's creation in the image and likeness of God informed his call for an egalitarian society. He was particularly critical of the institution of slavery, which he viewed as a grave sin against human dignity. By advocating for the abolition of slavery, Gregory laid the groundwork for later ecclesiastical and social movements aiming at liberation and equality.

The theological tenets of early Christian teachings on justice were also significantly shaped by the contributions of St. Augustine of Hippo. His seminal work "The City of God" juxtaposes the heavenly city, founded on divine love and justice, with the earthly city, characterized by self-love and injustice. Augustine contends that true justice is achievable only in God's Kingdom, yet he acknowledges the role of the Church in striving to implement divine principles within the temporal realm. His reflections on the nature of ownership and the common good continue to inform Catholic social teaching to this day.

Building upon these foundations, the early monastic communities also played a pivotal role in embodying and propagating the principles of social justice. St. Benedict of Nursia's "Rule," which became the cornerstone of Western monasticism, emphasizes communal living, mutual support, and the equitable distribution of resources. Benedictines were often at the forefront of agricultural innovation, education, and charitable activities, acting as living testimonies to the application of the Church's social doctrines. Through their vow of poverty, they modeled a tangible renunciation of material excess, advocating instead for a life of simplicity and communal well-being.

Moreover, the socio-political context of the early Church significantly shaped its teachings on justice. Living in a period of Roman imperial rule, early Christians frequently found themselves at odds with societal norms and structures that perpetuated inequality and exploitation. The Christian denunciation of infanticide, gender injustice, and gladiatorial combat were all early manifestations of its commitment to the sanctity of life and the inherent dignity of every person—principles firmly rooted in social justice.

It is essential to underscore that the early Church's commitment to social justice was not merely theoretical but practical and communal. The Acts of the Apostles describes the earliest Christians as holding "all things in common" (Acts 4:32), a vivid depiction of economic solidarity. This practice, although not without its challenges, illustrates their profound commitment to a just and equitable community, anticipating later theological developments and Church councils that would further articulate and codify these ideals.

The writings and practices of the early Church Fathers laid the groundwork for a rich tradition of Catholic social teaching that has evolved through the centuries. They exemplify a profound synergy between faith and action, urging believers to manifest God's justice within the world. Their contributions continue to resonate, offering a timeless testament to the enduring power of the Church's commitment to social justice.

Their legacy forms an unbroken chain within the tapestry of Catholic doctrine, binding past, present, and future generations in a solemn commitment to uphold the dignity, rights, and responsibilities that constitute true justice. As we glean from their profound wisdom, we are reminded that the quest for social justice is not a mere adjunct to our faith, but its very heart, summoning us to a higher calling—to live out the Gospel in both word and deed, in the pursuit of God's everlasting justice.

Developments through Church History

As the annals of history unfurl, one can discern the unwavering dedication of the Church to the pursuit of social justice. From the dawning of Christianity through the medieval era, the Renaissance, and into the modern age, the Church's teachings and actions have evolved, contextualizing the perennial quest for righteousness within the ever-changing fabric of society. Indeed, the Church has never wavered in its commitment, always seeking to balance divine principles with human exigencies.

In the nascent years of the Church, the Apostolic Fathers grappled with the pagan world's disparate values. Their writings echo the fundamental tenets of justice and mercy that Christ Himself promulgated. The Epistle of Barnabas and the Didache are prime illustrations, emphasizing communal sharing and support for the vulnerable. These early texts laid the groundwork for a Christian ethos that regards social equity not as a mere preference, but as an imperative.

Moving into the early Middle Ages, the intellectual beacons such as St. Augustine of Hippo began to craft a more structured theological framework. Augustine's magnum opus, "De Civitate Dei" (The City of God), juxtaposes the temporal city of man with the eternal city of God, each with its own conception of justice. Augustine posited that true justice is impossible without recognition of divine order, an argument that resonated through centuries and continues to inform Catholic thought on social justice.

As the curtain rose on the High Middle Ages, the scholastics further advanced these dialogues. St. Thomas Aquinas, in his seminal work "Summa Theologica," elaborated on natural law, emphasizing that human laws must align with divine law to be just. Aquinas' intricate synthesis of Aristotelian philosophy and Christian doctrine provided a robust ethical framework that underscored the importance of moral rectitude and social responsibilities.

In the Renaissance and Reformation periods, the Church faced significant challenges, both theological and socio-political. The Humanist movement, with its emphasis on the dignity and potential of the individual, found resonance within Catholic circles. Prominent figures like Erasmus of Rotterdam advocated for educational and ecclesiastical reforms, stressing that true social justice could only be achieved through a more humane and enlightened society.

The post-Reformation era saw the Catholic Church respond to growing societal complexities with renewed vigor. The Council of Trent (1545–1563) was a pivotal moment, as it sought to address corruption and reform Church practices, reinforcing the importance of moral and social justice. The decrees of the Council not only aimed at spiritual renewal but also mandated practical measures to care for the poor and marginalized.

The Enlightenment presented both challenges and opportunities. Enlightenment philosophers often critiqued the Church, yet their emphasis on reason and individual rights unwittingly echoed long-standing Christian teachings on human dignity and justice. The Church, especially through the writings of figures like Bishop Jacques-Bénigne Bossuet, articulated a response that sought to harmonize faith and reason, emphasizing that true justice is rooted in divine wisdom.

In the 19th century, facing the rise of industrialization and the associated social upheavals, the Church's voice on social justice became more pronounced. Pope Leo XIII's encyclical "Rerum Novarum" (1891) is particularly noteworthy. This seminal document addressed the conditions of the working classes and outlined the rights of workers and the responsibilities of employers, thus laying the groundwork for modern Catholic social teaching. Leo XIII underscored that the pursuit of justice is inseparable from Christian charity and moral duty.

The 20th century witnessed continued development in the Church's social doctrine, addressing emerging issues such as global conflicts, economic disparity, and human rights. The Second Vatican Council (1962-1965) was a watershed moment, emphasizing the Church's role in the modern world. The Council's Pastoral Constitution "Gaudium et Spes" underscored the

Church's commitment to human dignity and the common good, urging Catholics to engage actively in societal transformation.

Subsequent papal encyclicals, such as "Pacem in Terris" by Pope John XXIII and "Populorum Progressio" by Pope Paul VI, expanded on these themes, advocating for peace, development, and the elimination of institutional injustices. These documents highlighted the Church's proactive stance in addressing the root causes of social ills and promoting systemic changes in alignment with Christian ethics.

Recent decades have seen the papacy of St. John Paul II, whose extensive writings further enriched the Church's social teaching. His encyclicals "Laborem Exercens," "Centesimus Annus," and "Evangelium Vitae" amalgamate theological and philosophical insights to tackle modern dilemmas. John Paul II championed the sanctity of human life, the rights of workers, and the imperative for social systems that foster genuine human flourishing.

Pope Benedict XVI and Pope Francis have continued this legacy, addressing contemporary issues such as environmental degradation, economic inequality, and global migration. Benedict XVI's "Caritas in Veritate" (Charity in Truth) calls for an economy that serves the human person, while Pope Francis's "Laudato Si'" (On Care for Our Common Home) broadens the scope of social justice to include ecological concerns, urging the care of creation as an integral part of faith.

In sum, the Church's historical engagement with social justice reflects a dynamic interplay between immutable divine precepts and the mutable circumstances of human existence. This historical journey underscores a fundamental truth: social justice, in the Catholic tradition, is both a divine mandate and a human endeavor, ever evolving, closely intertwined with theological developments, and responsive to the exigencies of each era. Through its steadfast commitment, the Church continues to illuminate the path towards a just and compassionate world.

Chapter 11: Contemporary Issues in Social Justice

As we traverse the manifold currents of the present age, the endeavor to align temporal societies with the tenets of Catholic Social Justice attains renewed significance. The modern epoch, fraught with unparalleled vicissitudes, beckons the soul to wrestle with pernicious inequities and systemic failings that rend the fabric of moral order. These issues, ranging from the blights of poverty and inequality to the tumult of racial and environmental injustices, implore a divine reckoning harmonized with human action. Within the contemporary tableau, the voice of the Church emerges as a harbinger of erudition, offering sagacious frameworks imbued with theological profundity. The coalescence of doctrine with praxis demands an unwavering commitment to the sanctity of human dignity and the common good, transcending ephemeral political fancies to seek solutions rooted in the eternal verities of faith. Thus, the ecclesiastical response to contemporary social justice challenges delineates a luminous path, whereby the sacred and the secular interplay to uphold the immutable principles of justice, equity, and divine charity.

Modern Social Justice Challenges

In the swirling maelstrom of today's society, the challenges to achieving social justice have become abundantly complex and multifaceted. The world, with its technological advancements and global interconnectedness, has unveiled not only new opportunities but also nuanced issues that beckon for resolution. Our discourse here shall endeavor to elucidate these contemporary dilemmas whilst marking their resonance with the venerable principles of Catholic doctrine.

Firstly, we must address the pernicious issue of economic inequality. Wealth disparity has been an age-old conundrum, but its current incarnation presents unique strains upon the moral fabric of society. As the rich accrue wealth at an increasingly rapid pace, the poor find themselves ensnared in the relentless vice of poverty. The Catholic tradition, which espouses the principles of human dignity and the common good, impels us to challenge systems that perpetuate such inequities. Not only does economic inequality breed social unrest, but it also contravenes the Church's exhortation to prioritize the needs of the impoverished, a tenet deeply embedded in both scripture and doctrine.

The issue of racial injustice continues to plague our modern milieu. Despite significant strides toward equality, racial discrimination and systemic biases remain entrenched in various societal structures. The ripples of such deep-seated prejudice manifest in innumerable facets of life, from education to employment, and criminal justice. Catholic social teaching, which heavily underscores the inherent worth of every human being, finds such racial inequities abhorrent. It summons all believers to actively engage in the work of eradicating these injustices, thereby affirming the unity and sanctity of humankind.

Environmental degradation presents yet another formidable challenge to our generation. The accelerating climate crisis threatens not only the natural world but also imperils the most vulnerable among us. It is the poor and marginalized who suffer the brunt of ecological neglect and exploitation. Here, Catholic social justice impels us toward stewardship of creation, an idea outlined in the venerable documents of the Church, such as "Laudato Si'." This encyclical reminds us of our divine mandate to safeguard the earth, for it cries out alongside the marginalized in a hymn for justice.

Digital privacy and surveillance mark a relatively novel quandary in the canon of social justice challenges. As technology has become an inseparable part of daily life, questions about the ethics of data collection and surveillance have surged to the forefront. The Catholic Church's emphasis on human dignity and the inviolability of personal privacy intersects with these concerns. Intrusive surveillance mechanisms not only infringe upon individual rights but also inhibit the flourishing of a truly just society.

Immigration and the plight of refugees remain significant issues. The mass displacement of individuals due to war, persecution, and economic hardship demands a compassionate and just response. The Church teaches that every person, regardless of their nationality or legal status, deserves to be treated with dignity and respect. The modern challenge lies in reconciling this moral imperative with political and economic realities, calling upon leaders and laypeople alike to advocate for just and humane policies.

Gender inequality, too, persists as an anathema to the notion of social justice. Despite advancements, women continue to face discrimination and violence in myriad forms. The Catholic social teaching on human dignity asserts that men and women possess equal worth and are deserving of the same rights and opportunities. Thus, the contemporary struggle for gender justice necessitates a commitment to dismantling patriarchal structures that hinder the full flourishing of women in every sphere of life.

Political corruption and the erosion of democratic institutions are further modern-day challenges that cannot be ignored. When those in power subvert the legal and moral frameworks that hold them accountable, the foundation of a just society is imperiled. Catholic teaching calls for integrity, transparency, and accountability in public life, urging the faithful to be vigilant stewards of the common good and advocates for ethical governance.

Healthcare access and affordability emerge as critical issues in our times. The disparity in healthcare quality and the prohibition of access to medical necessities due to economic constraints starkly contradict the Church's advocacy for the right to life and the wholeness of the human person. Catholic doctrine insists on the preferential option for the poor, a principle which demands that healthcare systems be reformed to better serve the needs of all, particularly the most vulnerable.

Lastly, the crisis of social isolation and mental health represents an underappreciated yet deeply troubling challenge of contemporary society. With the advent of social media and the breakdown of traditional community structures, many individuals find themselves adrift in loneliness and despair. The Church's message of communion and solidarity offers hope and a remedy for this modern malaise. By fostering genuine communities of support and care, we can address the profound human need for connection and companionship.

In summation, these modern social justice challenges demand from us a renewed commitment to the timeless principles of Catholic teaching. They call upon us to apply the enduring truths of human dignity, the common good, and moral responsibility to the unfolding complexities of our age. As we navigate these turbulent waters, let us draw strength from our rich heritage and strive to build a world that more closely mirrors the divine justice and love enshrined in the Gospel.

Catholic Solutions to Contemporary Problems

As temporal society confronts an array of modern-day quandaries, it is incumbent upon the faithful to provide solutions that are not only just but also firmly grounded in Catholic teachings. The convergence of Persistent moral values and the exigencies of the present age renders a fertile ground for dialogue and action. Therefore, let us dissect these prevailing issues through the prism of Catholic social doctrine, elucidating a path towards a resplendent and equitable society.

An initial cornerstone in addressing contemporary dilemmas lies in reaffirming human dignity, the bedrock of Catholic ethics. Social injustices, from systemic poverty to racial discrimination, undermine the sanctity of the human person. To combat these malaises, the Church must advocate for policies that uphold the inherent dignity of every individual. This calls for an unwavering opposition to practices such as human trafficking, unfair labor practices, and any form of exploitation. Each person, bearing the image of God, deserves to be treated with respect and equity.

Further, in addressing economic disparities, Catholic theology offers the principle of the preferential option for the poor. Rooted in the Gospel teachings, this principle urges the more affluent sectors and governing bodies to prioritize the needs of the marginalized. By fostering initiatives aimed at alleviating poverty, such as equitable access to education and healthcare, the Church can play a pivotal role in mitigating economic imbalances. Such efforts not only reflect Christ's concern for the least of his brethren but also embody a tangible manifestation of love and justice in the world.

A pivotal aspect of the Church's response to contemporary issues also lies in environmental stewardship. The modern environmental crisis, characterized by climate change, loss of biodiversity, and rampant pollution, necessitates a robust moral and spiritual response. Pope Francis' encyclical *Laudato Si'* provides an invaluable guide by emphasizing the interconnectivity between humanity and nature. By advocating for sustainable living practices and policies that protect the environment, the faithful can manifest a reverence for God's creation, thus contributing to a holistic approach to social justice.

The fragmentation and polarization evident in today's political and social spheres pose additional challenges. To address these, the Church must emphasize the importance of solidarity and the common good. Through teachings that transcend partisan divides, Catholics can foster a culture of dialogue, mutual respect, and understanding. Community initiatives, ecumenical efforts, and interfaith dialogues all serve as conduits for building a cohesive and empathetic society. In an era marked by division, the Church stands as a beacon of unity and reconciliation.

In the realm of public health, recent global challenges such as pandemics have underscored the necessity of a compassionate and just healthcare system. Catholic social teaching underscores universal access to healthcare as a moral imperative, advocating for systems that ensure comprehensive care for all, irrespective of economic status. By supporting and participating in public health initiatives, the Church not only addresses immediate medical needs but also promotes the long-term well-being of communities.

Education remains another critical frontier where Catholic principles can be actualized. Quality education is a powerful tool for social mobility and empowerment. By championing educational initiatives that are inclusive and equitable, the Church can help bridge the gap between different socio-economic groups. In doing so, it nurtures individuals who are not only knowledgeable but also morally grounded, capable of contributing positively to society.

Contemporary issues also encompass the digital realm, where the rapid advancement of technology presents unique ethical challenges. From data privacy concerns to the moral implications of artificial intelligence, these issues necessitate a judicious application of Catholic ethics. By promoting digital literacy and ethical guidelines, the Church can guide individuals in navigating the complexities of the digital age while safeguarding human dignity and privacy.

Moreover, the safeguarding of life from conception to natural death is a perennial principle that must inform the Church's response to modern issues. In a cultural climate where practices such as abortion and euthanasia are often advocated under the guise of personal choice, the Church must resolutely uphold the sanctity of life. Supporting alternatives such as adoption, palliative care, and comprehensive support for expectant mothers and families enacts a culture of life and love.

Marriage and family, as the fundamental unit of society, face numerous contemporary threats, ranging from marital breakdowns to unconventional family structures. Catholic teaching provides a blueprint for strong and stable family units, emphasizing the sacramentality of marriage and the responsibilities therein. By fostering pastoral care, counseling services, and family support programs, the Church can help fortify family life, thus contributing to a healthier societal fabric.

Social justice also necessitates a focus on the rights and responsibilities of immigrants and refugees. In a world where displacement is a severe issue, Catholic teaching advocates for welcoming the stranger and offering sanctuary. Policies and practices that support the humane treatment of migrants, provide pathways to citizenship, and foster their integration into society are consistent with the Gospel's call to love one's neighbor.

The Church's voice in legal and political spheres must also be unambiguous and courageous. By engaging in advocacy for just laws and policies, Catholics can influence societal structures to reflect moral and ethical values. Arching back to the principles of natural law and the common good, the Church can guide lawmakers and politicians in crafting legislation that promotes justice and respects human rights. Its role is not merely passive but actively participatory in shaping a just society.

Additionally, the importance of peace and reconciliation in global conflicts cannot be overstated. The Church, embodying Christ's message of peace, must strive to be a mediator in war-torn regions. Promoting diplomatic solutions, supporting peace-building initiatives, and offering humanitarian aid align with the Church's mission of fostering global peace. This commitment to peace transcends national boundaries and calls for universal solidarity.

In sum, the Catholic response to contemporary problems, deeply rooted in theological and ethical foundations, offers a comprehensive blueprint for addressing the myriad issues facing modern society. By integrating principles of human dignity, the common good, preferential option for the poor, and unwavering commitment to justice and peace, the Church stands as a formidable force for positive transformation. Embodying these principles in every facet of societal life, Catholics can contribute to a world that mirrors the divine justice and mercy of God.

As we continue to grapple with the challenges of our time, let us remember that the tenets of Catholic social teaching are not static doctrines but living, dynamic principles that call us to action. Whether through policy advocacy, community initiatives, or individual acts of charity, each contribution is a step towards realizing a just and compassionate world. In the face of adversity, let our responses be guided by faith, reason, and unwavering commitment to the common good, for therein lies the true essence of Catholic solutions to contemporary problems.

Chapter 12: Practical Applications of Doctrine

In the realm of practical applications, one must endeavor to bridge the chasm 'twixt the lofty tenets of Catholic doctrine on social justice and their tangible manifestations within the labyrinth of quotidian existence. Herein, the symphony of divine decree harmonizes with the cacophony of human endeavor. The principles espoused by the Church, from the sanctity of human dignity to the pursuit of the common good, must metamorphose into actions that travail the realms of law, politics, and societal mores. Judges, attorneys, and politicians are called to hearken unto the moral imperatives enshrined within sacred teachings, wielding justice not merely as a legalistic construct but as a divine ordinance. Through the lens of real-world examples and case studies, both historical and contemporary, one perceives the resplendent tapestry of doctrine taking form in acts of compassion, equitable policies, and the unwavering advocacy for the marginalized. Thus, the eternal truths of faith find their ultimate expression in the concrete and corporeal acts of love, justice, and communal responsibility.

Implementing Social Justice Principles

The elucidation of social justice principles, as rooted in the rich tapestry of Catholic doctrine, necessitates the same ministerial zeal as the propagation of the Holy Gospel itself. Social justice, in this respect, transcends mere theoretical reverie, morphing into a robust praxis, guided by the venerable precepts handed down through generations.

To embody these principles, one must first comprehend the profound unity between rights and responsibilities. While the pursuit of justice might appear arduous, it stands as an integral manifestation of God's will, echoing through every Catholic's life like the tolling of sacred bells. In this sense, social justice is not a mere adjunct to faith but its very lifeblood, coursing through the actions of believers.

Legal professionals, politicians, and theologians must ponder the symbiotic relationship between divine command and human action. The challenge lies in marrying temporal governance with eternal truths, crafting policies and judgments that reflect the core tenants of Catholic social teaching. Judges, in particular, are tasked with interpreting laws through the lens of justice, embodying both the letter and the spirit of divine ordination.

Public officials and attorneys carry the torch of justice through their endeavors, ensuring that laws not only maintain order but espouse equity and compassion. These vocations are elevated from mere careers to sacred missions, echoing the ancient and everlasting precepts found within scripture and ecclesial tradition.

Politicians, too, are summoned to this noble purpose. Their policies must transcend partisan divides, drawing from the deeper wells of common good and distributive justice, as meticulously laid out in the Catechism. Enacting legislation that honors the dignity of each person, especially the marginalized, transforms governance into an act of divine stewardship.

Implementation within communities demands a collective awakening, a return to the vitality of early Church teachings where love of neighbor was paramount. Here, the parable of the Good Samaritan serves not as a quaint narrative but as a binding rubric for communal interaction. Love and justice must manifest in tangible actions, whether in charitable activities, advocacy for systemic change, or grassroots mobilization.

Faithful stewardship also requires rigorous catechesis and evangelization, ensuring the laity comprehends and acts upon these principles. Education becomes a beacon, guiding future generations to intertwine their faith with justice, understanding that both are inextricably linked and divine in origin.

Meanwhile, theologians must engage with contemporary socio-political debates, armed with natural law and theological ethics. Their exegesis and scholarly treatises should illuminate the path, showing that justice, rightly understood, heralds God's kingdom on earth, in alignment with salvific history.

A crucial element of implementing social justice principles is advocacy for the voiceless. Catholic doctrine mandates a preferential option for the poor, urging believers to champion their cause both in deed and policy. By doing so, Catholics reverently follow Christ's own predilection for the lowly and oppressed.

Furthermore, the delicate balance of justice and mercy finds embodiment in restorative justice practices. These practices restore both the offender and the victim to community, reflecting the divine image that both bear. This holistic approach mirrors the reconciliation that is central to Catholic sacraments and divine mercy.

Employing social justice principles demands unceasing vigilance against dehumanization in all its forms. Manifold issues such as poverty, racism, and environmental degradation must be met with the prophetic voice of the Church. Contemporary challenges, like the global refugee crisis, call for responses bathed in the spirit of the Good Shepherd—attentive, compassionate, and just.

In all these endeavors, the role of grace cannot be overstated. Divine grace emboldens believers to go beyond mere human efforts, allowing them to enact justice in ways that resonate with God's infinite love. Sacramental life, therefore, fuels the pursuit of social justice, ensuring that actions are not merely human endeavors but divine undertakings.

Ultimately, the praxis of social justice within Catholic doctrine threads the sacred with the secular, weaving a moral fabric that encompasses all aspects of life. The faithful are called to reflect the divine order in every realm—legal, political, social, and economic—thereby advancing the Kingdom of God through acts of justice and mercy.

Thus, the realization of social justice principles remains both a divine commandment and a testament to God's enduring covenant with humanity. As stewards of this divine charge, Catholics must continuously endeavor to manifest justice in all spheres, ensuring that God's justice is not merely an abstract ideal but a living reality.

In sum, the practical implementation of these principles requires an unwavering commitment to both faith and reason, an endeavor that calls for the collective effort of theologians, legal practitioners, politicians, and the laity. Through concerted actions and divine inspiration, the Church's vision of a just society ceaselessly unfolds, bearing witness to the incarnate love of Christ.

Case Studies and Real-World Examples

In elucidating the practical applications of Catholic social doctrine, the corpus of recorded history furnisheth us with numerous examples wherein the abstract principles of rights and responsibilities have been grounded in tangible deeds. These illustrations serve not merely to inspire, but to edify; they present a mosaic wherein the lofty canons of faith intertwine with the quotidian struggles of humanity. Here, we shall delve into case studies emblematic of such confluence.

Consider first the sanctified life and enduring legacy of Saint Damien of Molokai. His sojourn to the isolated leper colony on the Kalaupapa Peninsula of Molokai, Hawaii, stands as a resplendent testament to the moral imperatives expounded by Catholic doctrine. Saint Damien's sacrifice highlights the transcendent ideal that every human possesses intrinsic dignity, regardless of societal stigma or physical ailment. His unwavering commitment to the welfare of the abandoned lepers exemplifies the paramount duty to uphold human rights even at the expense of personal peril.

Another poignant portrait emerges with the tireless devotion of Dorothy Day, co-founder of the Catholic Worker Movement. Amidst the tumultuous milieu of the Great Depression, she pioneered the establishment of hospices, soup kitchens, and communal farms. Day's mission encapsulates the integration of Catholic social teaching and practical activism, particularly underscoring the Church's prerogative to engage with societal inequities. Her endeavors facilitate an understanding of how Catholic precepts on social justice can be operationalized to address systemic poverty and disenfranchisement.

The civil rights movement within the United States, notably the actions of Sister Thea Bowman, also offers rich insights. Sister Thea's indefatigable advocacy for racial equality and cultural inclusivity within the Catholic Church reverberates as a clarion call to justice. Her life's work demonstrates a profound blend of spiritual and social advocacy, urging the faithful to witness divine love through the pursuit of societal transformation. Her commitment to bridging the racial divide within ecclesiastical and civic realms furnishes a compelling archetype of the intersection between doctrine and activism.

Transitioning to the geopolitical realm, let us contemplate the remarkable interventions by the Catholic Church in the context of Latin America's liberation theology movement. Figures such as Archbishop Oscar Romero of El Salvador, martyred for his outspoken opposition to social injustices and state-sponsored violence, have become emblematic. Archbishop Romero's bold attainment of moral courage, borne out of his ecclesiastical duty, advocates that the Church's role is not mere bystander but active participant in the struggle for human rights and economic justice.

In the domain of peacemaking, the Council of Churches in Namibia (CCN) during the period of apartheid stands as a paragon. The solidarity and activism orchestrated by the CCN, heavily inspired by Catholic social teaching, rendered significant aid to the anti-apartheid struggle. The Church's involvement in these socio-political arenas elucidates a critical point: the doctrines on social justice and human rights transcend the walls of ecclesia, expanding into the broader societal fabric to spearhead concrete change.

It would be remiss to overlook the recent endeavors of Caritas Internationalis, a confederation of Catholic charity organizations. Their intricate work, providing humanitarian aid in the wake of natural disasters, refugee crises, and areas afflicted by conflict, upholds the quintessential Christian duty to "love thy neighbor." Caritas Internationalis embodies an organizational embodiment of doctrine, translating moral imperatives into structured, impactful actions that uphold and protect human dignity across the globe.

The phenomenon of restorative justice within the Catholic framework provides yet another salient illustration. Programs like those spearheaded by the Center for Restorative Justice Works in California underscore the union of doctrine with praxis. These initiatives seek to heal societal rifts caused by crime, fostering reconciliation and rehabilitation as opposed to mere retribution. Their success underscores a foundational tenet of

Catholic social justice—restorative justice reforms honor the dignity of all involved while seeking harmonious societal restoration.

Parallelly, the global advocacy against human trafficking pursued by the Church, prominently led by groups such as Talitha Kum, exemplifies a concentrated, doctrinal adherence to safeguarding the oppressed. These initiatives aggressively confront modern slavery, illustrating how ecclesiastical principles on human rights manifest in concerted action against profound human injustices. Their resolute stance embodies the Church's commitment to dismantling sin wrought through structural evils.

One must also reflect upon the ubiquitous influence of Catholic teaching in legislative and policy frameworks. Take, for instance, the transformation of Ireland's social policies in the late 20th and early 21st centuries. Grounded in Catholic ethical and social teaching, these policies were pivotal in guiding debates and eventual shifts on issues as diverse as healthcare, education, and labor rights. The moral persuasions emanating from the Irish episcopacy and laity contributed substantively to the shaping of national social policy, driving home the point that doctrine does not subsist in isolation but actively informs and molds the contours of civil governance.

Within the modern corporative environment, businesses inspired by Catholic social principles are not mere mythos. The implementation of fair wages, ethical labor practices, and environmental stewardship by Catholic-owned enterprises stands as a testament. Illustrative is the conglomerate Mondragon Corporation in Spain, which operates on cooperative principles deeply influenced by Catholic social teaching. Herein, labor is valorized, ownership is democratized, and operations are conducted with an eye towards the common good, reflecting doctrine's direct implications on economic structures.

Lastly, the advocacy for environmental stewardship as propounded in Pope Francis's encyclical *Laudato Si'* offers a contemporary glimpse into the Church's engagement with global crises. This doctrinal proclamation urges a holistic transformation towards sustainable living, deeply embedding the respect for creation within the rubric of social justice. Grassroots and international efforts stimulated by this encyclical have begun to foster ecological awareness and action, catalyzing a paradigm shift towards environmental ethics rooted in Catholic teaching.

In summation, these case studies and real-world examples firmly tether the abstract principles of Catholic doctrine to the lived realities of mankind. They elucidate that rights and responsibilities, articulated through the prisms of theology and apologetics, are not detached ethical aspirations but active, lived commitments. In their diversity, they lay bare the profound potential for doctrine to mobilize and manifest in societal praxis, transforming sacred ideals into palpable acts of righteousness. Through such exemplars, the Church continues its venerable mission, illuminating the path towards justice, dignity, and the common good for all creation.

Conclusion

The path traveled within the pages of this tome has indeed been a traversal through the intricate and profound realms of theology, philosophy, and social justice. In synthesizing these diverse domains, we have ventured to unveil the inherent unity between the notion of Catholic Social Justice and the apologetics for the existence of God. These pursuits, while seemingly disparate, converge upon a common axis signifying the divine order and human responsibility.

At the heart of Catholic Social Teaching lies an intricate balance of rights and responsibilities. This duality manifests itself through the principles that guide our moral compass and societal interactions. The Church, as a bastion of moral and spiritual guidance, propounds that the rights afforded to each individual are accompanied by corresponding responsibilities. It is through this harmonious relationship that justice is not merely a theoretical construct, but a lived experience grounded in the teachings of Christ and the traditions of the Church.

As we shift our gaze towards the realm of apologetics, the classical and contemporary arguments for the existence of God present themselves as more than mere intellectual exercises. Rather, they are foundational to understanding the moral imperatives that underpin our responsibilities. The acknowledgement of a divine creator who imbues every human being with inherent dignity and worth elevates the discourse on rights from a secular understanding to a sacred mandate. Each argument for God's existence, whether ontological, cosmological, or teleological, fortifies the conviction that our duties towards one another are divinely ordained.

The philosophical underpinnings of rights and responsibilities are not abstract musings, but concrete realities that echo the teachings of natural law. This moral order, perceived through reason and revelation, dictates that human rights are intrinsic and inviolable. Yet, these rights are incomplete without an attending recognition of moral duties, propelling us towards acts of justice and charity. Apologetics serves as the bridge that binds ethical imperatives to theological truths, underscoring our role as stewards of creation tasked with upholding justice.

Human dignity emerges as a pivotal theme within this discourse, a core principle that suffuses Catholic teaching. It is through the lens of dignity that we discern the moral directives of Scripture and the teachings of the Church. Our responsibilities to each other, to society, and to the Divine itself are reflections of this inherent dignity. It calls upon us to seek the common good, to advocate for the marginalized, and to cultivate a community rooted in the virtues of justice, prudence, and charity.

The concept of the common good serves as a clarion call within our theological and societal framework. Catholic teaching posits that the flourishing of the individual is inseparable from the welfare of the community. In navigating this relationship, we encounter the profound implications of natural law and moral order, compelling us to strive for a society that reflects the divine justice and compassion of God. Our personal and collective actions must be in pursuit of this ultimate good, as it forms the bedrock of a just and equitable society.

Scripture provides a rich tapestry of justice and social responsibility, grounding our theological understanding in the lived experiences of biblical figures and the teachings of Christ. The exhortations of the prophets, the parables of Jesus, and the epistles of the apostles all resonate with a call to justice, reminding us that our faith is intrinsically linked to our actions within the world. The scriptural basis for social justice reinforces our duties and rights, providing a divine mandate for the pursuit of righteousness.

The interplay of grace and free will introduces a theological paradox that enriches our understanding of human action and divine providence. Grace, as the unmerited favor of God, enables us to transcend our limitations and fulfill our moral duties. Simultaneously, free will empowers us to choose the good, to act justly, and to love mercy. This dynamic interplay affirms our capacity for moral agency, urging us to align our lives with the divine will and to embody the principles of justice and charity.

As we reflect upon the historical trajectory of social justice within the Church, we observe a continuum of teachings and practices that have evolved yet remained steadfast in their core principles. From the early Church Fathers to contemporary theologians, the pursuit of justice has been a perennial concern. The Church's response to modern social justice challenges is informed by this rich tradition, offering solutions that are both timeless and timely. Our engagement with contemporary issues, guided by Catholic teaching and tradition, provides a framework for addressing the complexities of the modern world.

The practical applications of doctrine, as illustrated through various case studies and real-world examples, demonstrate that the principles of Catholic Social Teaching are not merely theoretical but profoundly actionable. Implementing these principles requires a commitment to justice, a dedication to service, and a willingness to challenge systemic inequities. The real-world implications of our theological and philosophical insights compel us to live out the tenets of our faith in tangible ways, fostering a society that reflects the love and justice of God.

As we draw this exploration to a close, it is evident that the confluence of Catholic Social Justice and apologetics for the existence of God offers a robust framework for understanding our place within the divine economy. Our rights and responsibilities, grounded in the recognition of human dignity and the pursuit of the common good, are illuminated by the light of divine revelation and reason. This synthesis invites us to engage more deeply with our faith, to act justly, and to love mercy as we journey towards the fulfillment of God's kingdom on earth.

May we, in our varied capacities as theologians, judges, attorneys, politicians, and faithful believers, endeavor to uphold these principles with unwavering commitment. Let our actions reflect the divine harmony of justice and love, and may we be instruments of God's peace and justice in the world.

Appendix A: Appendix

In this appendix, we shall endeavor to elucidate the intricate yet harmonious convergence of the principles articulated herein. This compendium serves to augment the reader's understanding of the substantive connections interwoven between the manifold tenets of Catholic Social Justice and the doctrinal assertions of God's existence articulated through Apologetics. Through the synthesis of theological, philosophical, and moral doctrines, we discover an interlaced fabric that upholds the edifice of our shared human dignity and ethical responsibilities. Reflect upon these distilled insights as they offer a holistic view of our divine obligations and social imperatives, uniting the sacred with the empirical in a testament to our enduring quest for justice and truth.

Glossary of Terms

Apologetics - The theological discipline aimed at defending and explaining the faith, particularly the existence of God, through reasoned arguments.

Common Good - A principle referring to the benefit or interests of all individuals within society, which all members have a duty to promote and protect.

Dignity - The inherent worth and respect owed to every human being, grounded in the belief that all individuals are created in the image of God.

Grace - The free and unmerited favor of God, manifested in the salvation of sinners and the bestowal of blessings.

Moral Imperative - An essential duty or obligation rooted in ethical principles, often viewed as binding on all individuals regardless of personal inclination.

Natural Law - The doctrine that certain rights and moral values are inherent in human nature and discoverable through reason, often seen as the basis for ethical behavior and human rights.

Rights - Entitlements or permissions accorded to individuals, either by virtue of their human nature or by societal or legal frameworks; essential for the protection of human dignity and justice.

Responsibilities - Duties or obligations that individuals have towards others and society at large, often interlinked with rights, in Catholic teachings.

Social Justice - The virtue and practice of ensuring that all individuals receive their due from society, encompassing fair treatment, access to resources, and the protection of rights.

Tenet - A core principle or belief that is held as a foundational truth, particularly within a religious, philosophical, or moral framework.

Theological - Pertaining to the study of God, divine things, and religious beliefs; it provides a systematic exposition of the faith and its claims.

Bibliography

The pursuit of knowledge should always be coupled with reverence for those who have ventured into the realms of theological, philosophical, and legal discourse before us. Within this "Bibliography," we encompass a wealth of wisdom gleaned from various erudite sources, strictly curated to illuminate the expanse of Catholic Social Justice and Apologetics.

To commence, the foundation of this erudite endeavor is firmly established upon the ancient texts and scriptures that enkindle the tenets of Catholic thought. Notably, the Holy Bible stands as the paramount source, elucidating the principles of justice, grace, and the existence of the Divine. References to key biblical passages and the teachings enshrined within the New and Old Testament form the bedrock of this compendium.

The Church Fathers, whose luminescence continues to guide us, feature prominently in our exploration. Texts from St. Augustine's "City of God" and St. Thomas Aquinas's "Summa Theologica" offer unparalleled insight into the synthesis of faith and reason. These texts track the lineage of thought from the nascent Church up to the scholastic endeavors that resonate through centuries.

- *The Holy Bible*: Both the New and Old Testament – key biblical passages underpinning justice and responsibility.
- *City of God* by St. Augustine – profound theological reflections foundational to Christian philosophy.
- *Summa Theologica* by St. Thomas Aquinas – detailed expositions on natural law, moral order, and divine existence.

Delving into the corridors of history, the wisdom encapsulated in ecclesiastical documents such as Encyclicals and Papal Letters provides contemporary Church perspectives on social justice. Documents such as "Rerum Novarum", by Pope Leo XIII, and "Laudato Si'", by Pope Francis, articulate the Church's stance on modern issues, threading ancient wisdom with present exigencies. The library of England's Magdalen College and the Vatican Archives unfold cohorts of such papal writings.

Moreover, contemporary theological works also stand as pillars holding aloft the grand edifice of our understanding. Authors like G.K. Chesterton and Hans Urs von Balthasar offer modern exegeses and affirmations of the doctrines we hold dear. Their treatises bolster our grasp of the alignment between Catholic social doctrine and apologetic rationality.

Philosophical analysis, an indispensable companion in our quest for truth, is enriched by texts from formidable philosophers whose works resonate with the rhythms of Christian thought. Friedrich Nietzsche, notwithstanding his departure from theistic rigor, presents dialectics that sharpen our apologetic arguments. Similarly, detailed treatises from Immanuel Kant and John Stuart Mill broaden the discourse on natural law and moral imperatives. Through these writings, we engage in a grand dialectic exploring divine existence and the moral fabric of society.

- Papal Encyclicals and Apostolic Letters – including "Rerum Novarum" and "Laudato Si'".
- Writings of G.K. Chesterton – modern perspectives on social principles and apologetics.
- Philosophical works by Friedrich Nietzsche, Immanuel Kant, and John Stuart Mill – critical engagements with moral order and theological foundations.

To bind all these contemplations into a coherent tapestry, secondary sources such as peer-reviewed journal articles and critical essays provide invaluable support. Works from "Theological Studies" and "Journal of Catholic Social Thought" offer academic rigor and interpretative clarity. Scholarly interpretations and empirical studies conducted by institutions like the Pontifical Academy of Social Sciences and the American Catholic Philosophical Association infuse our discussion with precision and authority.

Judicial opinions and legal treatises that reflect Catholic social doctrine are integral. Esteemed legal scholars like John Finnis and Germain Grisez offer jurisprudential interpretations that connect divine law with human rights and societal responsibilities. Their jurisprudence illuminates our understanding of legislative processes and judicial decisions influenced by ecclesiastical teaching.

- Peer-reviewed journals such as "Theological Studies" and "Journal of Catholic Social Thought".
- Publications from the Pontifical Academy of Social Sciences and the American Catholic Philosophical Association.
- Legal writings by John Finnis and Germain Grisez – aligning ecclesiastical law with modern jurisprudence.

As we traverse the bridge connecting Catholic Social Justice and Apologetics, historical records also offer an essential compass. Chronicles from early Christian communities and medieval ecclesiastical courts shed light on the evolution of social doctrines and legal principles. Noteworthy are records from the Councils of Nicaea and Trent, as well as medieval legal codes like the "Decretum Gratiani", which interweave theological insights with emerging notions of justice.

In the pursuit of compiling such a comprehensive bibliography, a diligent discerning eye ensures that the sources exhibit veracity, scholarly fidelity, and relevance to the thematic essence of the book. This sensorium of knowledge nurtures an expansive understanding, enabling the reader to perceive the intrinsic interrelation between rights, responsibilities, and the existence of the Divine from a Catholic vantage.

- Historical ecclesiastical records – Councils of Nicaea and Trent, "Decretum Gratiani".
- Chronicles from early Christian communities and medieval ecclesiastical courts.

In summation, the "Bibliography" stands not merely as a log of readings but as a testament to an intellectual pilgrimage. Each text, each author undoubtedly flavors the discourse with their unique insights, rendering a harmonious confluence of tradition, philosophy, and living theology. Such a collation endeavors to fortify the reader's voyage through the intricate expanse of Catholic social justice and apologetic wisdom, sailing steadfast under the aegis of informed faith and reason.